How to Design & Build Fences & Gates

Created and Designed by the Editorial Staff of Ortho Books

Project Editor
Kathleen Blease

Writer
Jeff Beneke

Illustrator
Pamela Drury Wattenmaker

Ortho Books

Publisher
Robert B. Loperena
Editorial Director
Christine Jordan
Managing Editor
Sally W. Smith
Editors
Robert J. Beckstrom
Michael D. Smith
Prepress Supervisor
Linda M. Bouchard
Sales & Marketing Manager
David C. José
Publisher's Assistant
Joni Christiansen
Graphics Coordinator
Sally J. French

Consultants
Larry Haun
Scott Whitham
Editorial Coordinator
Cass Dempsey
Copyeditor
Melinda E. Levine
Proofreader
David Sweet
Indexer
Frances Bowles
Separations by
Color Tech Corp.
Printed in the USA by
Banta Book Group
Thanks to
Phyllis Calech
Deborah Cowder
The Elizabeth F. Gamble
  Garden Center
David Van Ness
Andrea Voinot

Photographers
William Aplin: 9BR, 48–49,
  back cover BL
Laurie Black: 11T, 11B,
  17BL, 18
John Blaustein: 7BR
Alan Copeland: 50
Wendy Cortesi: 72
Crandall & Crandall: 3T, 3B,
  4–5, 7BL, 8TL, 9BL, 10T,
  10BL, 10BR, 17TR, 17BR,
  81TL, 81TR, 81B
David Goldberg: 6T, 19B,
  back cover TL
Susan Lammers: 6B, 7T
Michael McKinley: 19T,
  back cover BR
Douglas Muir: 16T
John Neubauer: 8TR
Geoff Nilsen: 17TL
Ortho Photo Library: 9T,
  80L, 82L
Gay Bumgarner, Photo/
  NATS: 16B, back cover TR
Kenneth Rice: Front cover
Mark Turner: 1, 8B, 78–79,
  80R, 82R

Builders
Janan Apaydin, Apaydin
  Ecoscapes: 6T
David Helm: 1, 78–79,
  80R, 82R

Front Cover
This attractive fence clearly benefits the owner, but it is also a gift to the neighborhood. It graces the sidewalk and sends a cheerful message to all who pass.

Title Page
Fences and gates provide abundant opportunities to practice woodworking skills. Fabricating the complex trusses of this pergola and cutting the curved members of the gate required careful craftsmanship.

Page 3
Whether part of an elegant front entry (top) or a private backyard retreat (bottom), fences and gates are important for defining spaces, marking boundaries, and providing a link between the garden and the built environment.

Back Cover

Top left: This gate has many of the same architectural details used on buildings, such as the pedimental top and applied moldings.

Top right: The natural wood color of this fence blends nicely with the garden.

Bottom left: Although fence construction is fairly basic, keeping the fence straight, plumb, and level requires careful craftsmanship.

Bottom right: Fences don't have to be all business. This design from a bygone era is conducive to restful enjoyment.

Address all inquiries to:
Ortho Books
Box 5006
San Ramon, CA 94583-0906

© 1985, 1997 Monsanto Company
All rights reserved

2 3 4 5 6 7 8 9
98 99 2000 01 02

ISBN 0-89721-320-3
Library of Congress Catalog Card
Number 96-67950

THE SOLARIS GROUP
2527 Camino Ramon
San Ramon, CA 94583-0906

How to Design & Build Fences & Gates

DESIGNING FENCES

Everyone needs boundaries—to seclude, to surround, to protect, to define limits. Fences help fulfill that need with strong physical boundaries or gentle visual ones. They mark where one world or activity ends and another begins, providing safety, comfort, and reassurance.

Though a fence is a simple structure, it has visual impact and can play a significant part in creating an impression for your property. When it is carefully planned, designed, and constructed, a fence can be strikingly beautiful, no matter how simple or complex its style, adding comfort and value to your home and property. The expenditure of energy, time, and money can yield a tremendous return.

Regardless of the level of your hands-on involvement, the more you know about quality in materials, construction, and maintenance, the better equipped you will be to make the right choices. In the end, you'll have just the fence you need, and its durability will remind you that careful planning, not ignorance, is bliss.

The primary purpose of this fence is to provide privacy and security, but it accomplishes so much more. A few details transform it from an ordinary board fence into an attractive showpiece. Notice how the gracefully curved top, decorative finials, and neutral color scheme contribute to a serene, stylish feeling, while the bench, mailbox, and intercom help identify the concealed gate.

WHY A FENCE?

There is a long history of fence building—a tradition that extends from the depths of the wilderness to the breadth of the plains; from the farm's back forty to the half-acre suburban homesite or the tiniest garden on a city lot.

What are your reasons? Rank them in order of their importance and in order of their ability to improve your situation.

The photographs on these pages show examples of fences in action. They illustrate the principles of function at work. You'll see that, depending on its design, a fence can serve several purposes. As you look at the photographs, list your own priorities and keep them in mind as you decide the location and style of your fence.

Function First

Every fence that was ever built, no matter what its style, had a purpose, a job to do—perhaps several jobs at once. The circumstances that prompted fence building in other times and other places may have differed from those we face today, but at the heart of all these circumstances lies a basic human need that motivates us to build fences.

In order to build the right fence—one that serves your purpose—it is important to clarify your needs. Put the issue of style aside for the moment. The first questions to ask yourself are functional ones: What is the purpose of the fence? What problems do you want it to solve? What are the needs of your household? How can a new fence improve the site? In short, what are your practical goals?

• To create privacy?
• To highlight a view or screen out an unattractive one?
• To define a special area?
• To provide security and protection for people, pets, and property?
• To buffer the effects of climate or noise?
• To enhance the appearance and increase the value of your property?

These are the basic reasons why most people build fences.

These five fences share a common purpose—to mark property boundaries and provide security—but each fence accomplishes this goal in a particular way that is appropriate to its setting.

Opposite page: Top: A wooden fence blends with the natural setting of this garden. The solid boards create privacy and protection, but its stepped design and the open spaces created by the top rail prevent the fence from becoming a visual barrier as well. Bottom: An iron fence provides security and a sense of decorum to this front yard without masking the view.

This page: Top: Any fence this long would call attention to itself, especially in such a prominent corner location. So why not be bold and build an eye-catching white picket fence? It is low enough to provide safe sight lines. The classic design creates a feeling of familiarity, and the repetition of forms sets up a pleasing rhythm. Bottom left: This stockade fence doesn't offer complete privacy from the massive building behind it, but its vertical lines and solid form give a strong sense of protection. Bottom right: Here, a playful and whimsical design creates a dance-like effect.

Opposite page: Top left: This 8-foot-tall fence provides maximum privacy without appearing to tower over the garden. The scalloped top, thin trim boards, and airy lattice pattern prevent the fence from feeling like a solid wall. Top right: This fence of lattice panels, also 8 feet tall, demonstrates how the color of a see-through fence influences its impact. Subdued colors, unlike white, allow objects beyond the fence to be seen through it, thus enlarging the perceived space. Bottom: Like a picture frame around a painting, this fence provides a tidy, restrained border around the flower bed.

This page: Top: A custom metal fence echoes the spare, stark lines of this contemporary-style home. Bottom left: A simple grid of 1×2s adds depth and substance to this fence, giving it an architectural presence of its own. Bottom right: Swimming pools must be fenced to keep toddlers and stray animals from venturing too close.

Top: The fence and gates around this garden add to its breathtaking beauty in many ways. By defining the space, they highlight the lush lawn and stunning begonias. The fence and gates are also attractive features themselves. The relatively simple fence design, with a few refined embellishments, reinforces the serenity and order of the garden. Certain details, such as the circular openings in the gates, add interesting focal points. Overall, the fence and gates establish a delightful interplay between the visitor and the garden by simultaneously framing views that invite one to pause and linger, and extending views that beckon one to move on and explore.

Bottom left: A solid panel fence is an effective way to block noise from a busy street. For maximum sound control and privacy, there should be no openings, and all joints should be tight. In this fence, the boards are locked into grooves milled along the sides of the posts. The finials and pediments across the top of the fence and the restful color prevent the fence from being drab and intrusive..

Bottom right: There's no rule that requires grapestakes to be installed vertically. Here, the horizontal fencing adds to the relaxed, rustic feeling of the deck, and provides an excellent buffer against annoying breezes.

Is a fence part of the house or part of the garden? A tall lattice fence (top) shapes and defines two distinct areas of this yard, but it also enhances the home. It is large enough not to be dwarfed by the grand scale of the house. Its curved shape, white color, square grid pattern, and decorative post tops echo various details of the home's facade. Vines soften the fence and help anchor it to the garden. A concealed gate bolsters privacy.

Bottom: A white picket fence blends perfectly with the architecture of this colonial home. Overall, the fence has a low, horizontal profile that reflects the building's proportions. At the same time, the slender pickets and pointed posts align with vertical features of the home's facade. The fence also has a light and open feeling that contrasts nicely with the dark brick exterior of the house.

WHERE TO PUT THE FENCE?

Your priorities and the site itself work together to help you decide where to locate the fence line. The site has a set of givens—some are features you like and want to retain, others are features you might wish to improve if you had the chance. A new fence will give you that chance.

Transforming Your Site

By discovering for yourself what the givens are (see the illustration on the opposite page), and by planning the new fence line carefully, you will find that your fence can transform your site in many pleasing ways. There are two approaches to planning your fence line. They are equally effective, so choose the one that is easier for you.

One approach is to plan it out on paper, using a site plan of your property as a base drawing and tracing-paper overlays to try out alternative fence-line schemes. Planning with pencil and paper is the fastest and easiest way to arrive at a pleasing result, but you need a site plan to do this. You can draw one in an hour or two, or you can try to find a copy of an existing site plan. If yours is a newer home or one that was specially designed, or if your property has had professional landscape work done, contact the appropriate sources—the building department, the designer or architect, the building contractor, the landscape contractor, or even the previous owner—to see if you can locate an existing plan.

The other approach is to plan your fence line right on the property itself; use stakes and string to create a temporary fence line, positioning and repositioning the mock-up until you are satisfied with the location. Then leave your stake-and-string fence in place for a few days or weeks; live with it long enough to know for certain that it is right. Experiment with alternative layouts, and by all means, seek out the opinions of others—especially family members and neighbors.

Establish Your Layout Priorities

Your priorities can help suggest a rough outline for the fence line. Where is it needed to do the job you want it to do? Read your list of priorities and ask yourself *Where?* for each one. Then jot down your answer. If you keep in mind who the fence is for—your pet, your child, your neighbor—you will have a good starting point.

Next, take a look at your home and property from three perspectives: from inside the house, from the outdoors, and from the neighborhood beyond your property lines. As you do so, ask yourself the following questions:

Guidelines for Planning Gate Openings

In addition to the gate design and construction considerations discussed on pages 82 to 91, there are some functional issues you will want to consider as you plan the width of gate openings. For foot traffic, an opening 3 feet wide is just big enough for a person and a large piece of equipment to pass through comfortably. A 4-foot-wide opening is a more comfortable minimum; and a 6-foot-wide opening will accommodate several people.

For vehicular traffic, make the opening 10 to 12 feet wide. The best way to get a sense of how wide the opening should be is to measure out a couple of options and see how comfortable the access is.

•What are the givens—those features you like and want to retain, and those you don't like and want to improve or camouflage?

•Where are the activity areas? What are they used for?

•What are the traffic patterns—from the street to the house, from the house to the outside areas, and from one area to another?

•How wide should openings in the fence be to accommodate these traffic paths?

•What surrounding views would you like to retain?

•Which views into your property would you like to block?

•What areas on the site would you like to mask or conceal, and from what vantage point?

•What is the direction of prevailing winds that you'd like to block or soften?

•What is the source of noise you'd like to exclude?

•Where does the sun rise and set in relation to your property?

A good way to get an overview of these issues is to map them out on a site plan.

On a tracing-paper overlay, draw circles for activity areas, arrows for traffic paths, wavy lines for winds, and so on. Such a map of your property helps you see how these issues affect the placement of the fence. After studying this map, you can plot the fence line with full confidence that it will accomplish your goals.

Investigate Building Codes and Property Lines

Like it or not, many other voices will have a say in your fence-building plans. The legal considerations that go hand in hand with most building projects are important and cannot be ignored.

Building Codes

Many communities have established building codes that define basic design and construction requirements for fencing. Some states have established height limits on residential fences; and historical districts may have strict

How to Draw a Site Plan

1. Make a sketch of your lot. Include the property lines, the house, driveway, patios, walkways, garden beds, and any other features you want to see on the completed plan.

   2. Take field measurements. Use a helper to hold the other end of a 50- or 100-foot tape. Measure the perimeter of the site, recording the dimensions on your sketch as you go. Measure whatever features you have included on your sketch.

   3. Transfer field measurements to ¼-inch-scale graph paper. Plot out the property lines. Locate and sketch in all the other site features you measured. Work lightly in pencil. When everything is in place and the site is visually represented, go back and darken the lines. If you note dimensions and the distances between elements on your site plan as you draw it, you will save yourself the time later of counting out squares to calculate distances. Keep in mind that this drawing need not look like an architect did it; if it is accurate and legible to you, it will serve your purposes just fine.

Sketching the Site

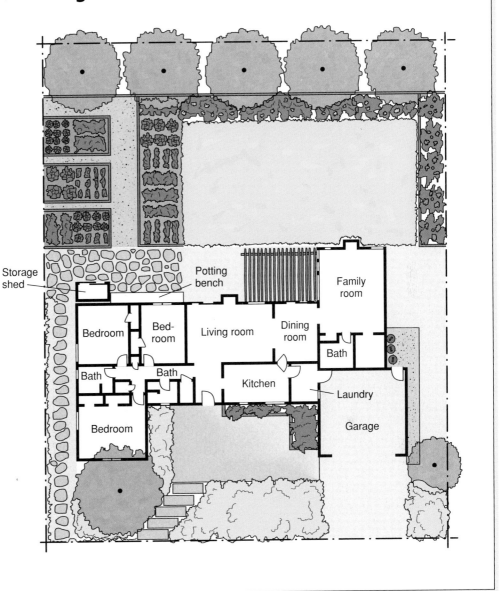

rules regarding styles and materials. Your local code may facilitate your planning by specifying the depth to which posts must be set, the width of gates, and the size of lumber.

   The primary purpose of building codes is to ensure that individual actions don't infringe on the rights of others—rights to bodily safety, fresh air, and unobstructed views. These codes also protect the environment and the public good. Building codes are the result of the legal compromises we make to ensure the common good.

   To find out what, if any, requirements or restrictions will pertain to the new fence, call the local building department. If there are good reasons to relax the requirements in favor of your plans, the building department can tell you how to apply for a variance. The aim of the department is to be of service; and the advice, help, and guidance are free.

Property Lines

It is important that you know the location of your property lines. If any part of the new

How Your Site Works

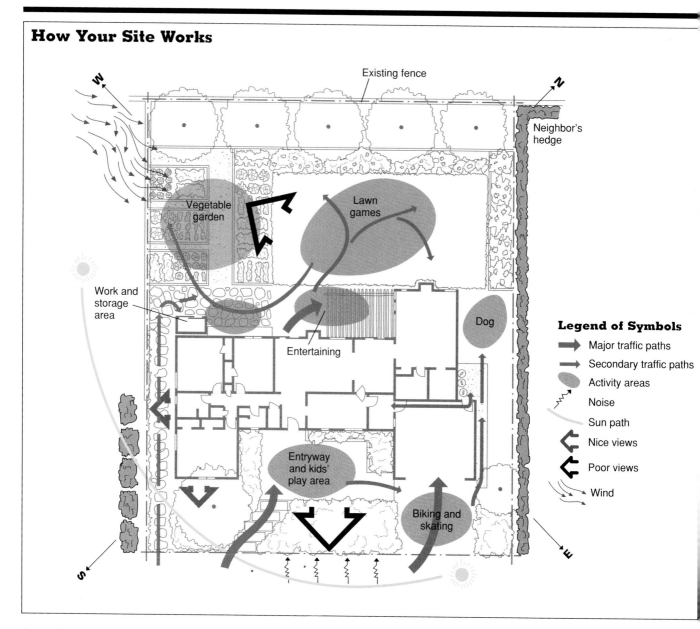

Existing fence

Neighbor's hedge

Vegetable garden

Lawn games

Work and storage area

Entertaining

Dog

Entryway and kids' play area

Biking and skating

Legend of Symbols

- Major traffic paths
- Secondary traffic paths
- Activity areas
- Noise
- Sun path
- Nice views
- Poor views
- Wind

fence should encroach on your neighbor's property, you will be the one responsible for moving it if your neighbor objects. Unless you and your neighbor jointly own and share responsibility for the fence (specified in writing), the new-fence installation must be wholly within the bounds of your own property, concrete footings included. You may be required to maintain *setback stipulations,* the distances the

fence must be kept away from adjacent property lines or from the street. If you live on a corner, the fence will not be allowed to restrict the view of motorists, for example.

Finding legal property lines can be tricky. Although you may be able to locate markers, such as wooden stakes or a pile of stones, you can't be sure that they haven't been moved over the years. In many instances, you will be

able to locate the boundaries from a survey map—which might be on file with the lending institution that handles your mortgage—or at your local building department. Alternatively, you may be able to locate the boundaries by following the written description of your property lines outlined in your deed. Your neighbor may help you to get a clear idea of where the boundaries are, but be aware

that this joint determination is a gentleman's agreement, not a legal settlement. If all else fails, consider having your site resurveyed (for a fee) by a surveyor or civil engineer.

Utilities

Do you know what's under the ground you want to dig up or fence over? If you aren't sure, find out if and where any electrical, natural gas, telephone, or plumbing lines are buried.

Plotting the Fence Line

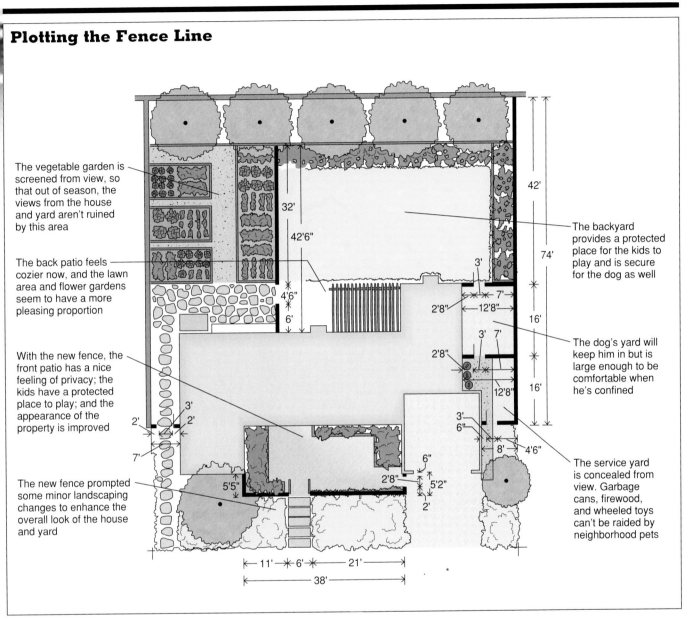

The vegetable garden is screened from view, so that out of season, the views from the house and yard aren't ruined by this area

The back patio feels cozier now, and the lawn area and flower gardens seem to have a more pleasing proportion

With the new fence, the front patio has a nice feeling of privacy; the kids have a protected place to play; and the appearance of the property is improved

The new fence prompted some minor landscaping changes to enhance the overall look of the house and yard

The backyard provides a protected place for the kids to play and is secure for the dog as well

The dog's yard will keep him in but is large enough to be comfortable when he's confined

The service yard is concealed from view. Garbage cans, firewood, and wheeled toys can't be raided by neighborhood pets

Contact the relevant utility companies and a plumber before finalizing your plans.

Make a Rough Layout

When you have a clear sense of the issues involved, try out some of them on paper or in the field to see how they look. Don't labor over any one layout scheme; in fact, you'll have more fun and find the best solution if you work freely and quickly. Dream a little. Use this book for ideas, or try some fanciful notion from your own imagination. This is how to get one idea to lead to another, and on to the actual plan. On the facing page, you'll see the basic rules of thumb for gates. For a fuller view of gate design considerations, see pages 82 to 91. Make a layout, stand back and look at it, and complete any necessary improvements. There are no hard and fast rules for creating a good fence line, but there are two ideals: Keep it simple and have it generously shape the outdoor space.

A simple straight fence, well designed and well built, has enough beauty in its own right to hold the eye. Fancy jogs in the fence line are distracting (and extra work) unless they serve a purpose.

By its own nature, outdoor space is expansive. Tight, stingy spaces make people feel boxed in, which is at odds with the natural feeling of the environment. Even service areas should be large enough so you can move comfortably around in them. And certainly, areas for outdoor living should feel ample and free.

Sketch the Layout

When your ideas have jelled and you've got the fence line where you want it, with gate openings sized and placed, make a sketch of the plan. If you are laying it out in the field, measure the distance of each length of fence and the width of each opening, and record the dimensions on a sketch. If you have been planning on paper from the start, make a sketch of the final plan on a fresh tracing-paper overlay and record the dimensions of the planned fence line.

This plan will be used to help you figure out the spacing between posts when you divide the line into bays (see pages 46 and 47), when you compute the materials you'll need, and when you actually stake the layout before beginning construction. (A *bay* is a section of fence running from one post to the next.)

Draw the Final Fence Line

To draw the final plan of the fence line, first tape a piece of tracing paper over the site plan. Then make a little circle where the boundary lines intersect (this makes it easy to get the overlay located again if you want to remove it and reposition it later). Draw out the fence layout you have in mind. Leave a break in the fence line to show where openings will be. If you plan to put a gate there, indicate the direction of the swing.

If in the course of making this sketch of your first idea you find there are things about the layout that you want to improve and change, jot down a few notes on the side of the tracing paper to remind you. Make as many sketches as you need.

Plotting the Fence Line

Let's look at the priorities of a certain household, for example. The new fence on this piece of property should:

• Provide protection (to keep neighborhood dogs out and the kids and the pet in the backyard)

• Create privacy (on the front patio)

• Shape and define space (around the back patio and lawn)

• Enhance the site (along the front of the property)

• Block noise (around the front patio)

• Conceal unsightly areas (near the garbage cans, work yard, and vegetable garden)

Top: Even an informal fence requires careful planning of its location, size, color, and other features. This variation of a Kentucky rail fence, painted white to give it a smart, crisp look, complements the rustic setting nicely. Bottom: Solid fences are best for some locations, open fences for others. This fence combines the two styles, capturing the best features of both.

Top and bottom: Both fences relate well to their sites because they use the same materials and finishes as adjacent structures.

Scale is an important element of fence design. Applying the lattice panels horizontally to full-length posts (top) keeps this sidewalk fence from being obtrusive. Bottom: Decorative lattice panels break up the broad expanse of this fence.

WHAT KIND OF FENCE?

Given your functional priorities, the issue of fence style begins to take on new meaning. The style you choose must serve two purposes: It should be visually appealing and it must meet your functional needs.

Wood or Metal?

This book focuses on designing and building fences that are made of wood, still the most popular material. Traditionally, the appearance of wood fences was distinctive and appealed more to the do-it-yourselfer; metal fences required the skills and tools of a professional to build. Today, however, that distinction between the styles and materials of wood and metal is blurring: Now products that mimic the appearance of one material are constructed of another material. For example, most of the standard styles of wood fences, from post-and-rail to picket, are now available in solid or veneered polyvinyl (PVC); and close replicas of wrought-iron fences are sold in steel or aluminum tubing. Mesh fencing can be found in metal, plastic, and plastic-coated metal. Purists may scoff at these imitations, but before passing judgment, realists may note the low-maintenance demands of PVC, or the greater affordability of aluminum. The "Resource Guide" on page 94 offers names and addresses of manufacturers of these newer fence systems.

Fence Styles

Starting on page 20, you will find a compendium of major fence styles that use a range of common materials. These illustrated descriptions will help you to compare different fence materials and styles, with regard to your own needs. As you look at the illustrations, keep your functional goals in mind. In addition, think about aesthetics from the broadest perspective. Consider how you want the new fence to relate to your existing site. Your home and property already express a certain design theme, a particular character. The features that make up this character are the architectural style of the dwelling and the nature of the landscaping. The fence, as a newcomer in this setting, will work best if it harmonizes with the established design themes.

Fences create a strong visual impression. In one setting, a certain type of fencing material in a particular style and finish can be a stunning complement to the property. In a different setting, the same fence might seem awkward and uncomfortably out of place.

Before selecting a specific style, decide how you want your fence to relate to your site. Should it be an extension of the house, a part of the

This low, open fence with wide gates helps to link the home with the entry walk.

garden, or a link between the two? Then use the illustrations on the following pages to help you answer the question, What kind of fence? In this chapter, you'll see for yourself how versatile fence styles can be. This versatility derives from the differences inherent in the building materials themselves (wood versus bamboo, vinyl versus metal) and from the way those materials are assembled to form the fence.

In most of the illustrations, the frame for each fence remains essentially the same except for changes in height. This helps you see both the aesthetic and functional characteristics of a fence and does not confuse the issue by including structural characteristics, as well. Structural variations can also make a big difference in the design of a fence (see page 36), although the choice of fencing material, or *infill*, has the most impact on the fence design.

Once you have chosen a basic style that appeals to you, you can use each illustration in another way. The construction details included are the actual specifications for that fence. The dimensions of one bay and each of its component parts are all you need to know to build that fence to any length, for any layout.

After you decide on a design, determine where to put the fence (pages 12 to 16). Next, you'll see how to negotiate slopes and obstructions (pages 41 to 43) and prepare for the construction (pages 50 to 55). Then, when you are ready to build, follow the actual instructions for building the fence, in the second chapter.

You can use the illustrated fence style as a basis for designing your own custom fence. Small variations in a fence's components make a big difference in its appearance. Experimenting with these variations and creating a special design can be as much fun as enjoying the finished product. To design your own fence, choose a fence style from the following pages, and then continue through the design sequence outlined on pages 35 to 40, choosing whatever design variations appeal to you. By the time you've finished your custom design, you might surprise yourself with your success. When you've completed the basic design, plan the fence layout, and complete the specifications for building (pages 43 to 47).

A garden fence can be a major feature of the landscape (top), or a quiet backdrop for plants (bottom).

Virginia Zigzag

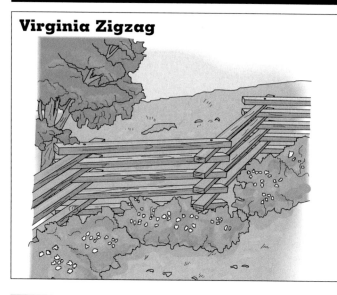

Kentucky Rail

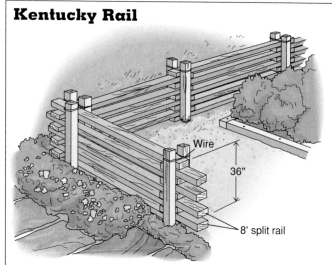

Wire

36"

8' split rail

Split Rail

Nails

48"

Rail Fence

The first American fences were built of wood from trees that were cleared to create fields. These fences, built from the heartwood of oak, chestnut, black locust, and cedar trees, could be expected to last up to one hundred years.

Today, such woods are in much shorter supply and they can be prohibitively expensive. Their place has been filled by pressure-treated softwoods, especially pine, fir, and hemlock. The styles have changed a bit as well, reflecting newer construction techniques and different fencing needs.

- •Protection and security: Moderate. Can impede access but is easy to climb over.
- •Visual privacy: Very little.
- •Tempering environment: Depending on style, can block drifting snow, but little else.
- •Defining space: Creates an informal, interesting boundary that can be bold and broad, or sparse and understated.
- •Suitable finish treatment: Let it weather naturally.

Rail Variations

The earliest American fence styles varied from region to region. They evolved with advances in milling techniques and construction practices, usually resulting in the need for less timber. In rural areas, fences were functional structures first and foremost.

Virginia Zigzag

Virginia zigzag fences were the most common choice of early American settlers. They were known also as

worm fences and as stacked-rail fences. Traditionally, this type of fence was made of saplings or rails split from larger logs, stacked in a simple zigzag pattern. This is still a beautiful style for lining a country road, though it does consume a large amount of wood. Lumber suppliers specializing in fencing materials sell split rails, but most often, they offer sawn rather than hand-split rails. Sawn rails don't have the same rustic appeal as split ones do. The rails are typically 8 feet long and of moderate cost; fence construction time is low.

Kentucky Rail

Kentucky rail fences, also known as double post-and-rail fences, evolved from the zigzag style. Their rails run straight and are held upright with confining posts on each side of the stack. They have the same rustic, rugged, and enduring look, and much of the beauty of the zigzag style, but take up less space and use less lumber. Construction time is low.

Split Rail

Split-rail fences grew out of the double-post system. Requiring only single posts at each rail junction, they simplified construction and used less wood. The main difference in the construction of this type of fence is that it is built one section at a time; you install one post, add the rails, then install another post. Depending on the purpose of the fence, you can vary the number of rails. Building suppliers sell posts and split rails ready for installation.

Mortised Rail

Nails

48"

Ranch Rail

Nails

48"

Capped Post-and-Rail

2×8

1×8

1½" 36"

1×4

1×8

Post-and-Board Fence

When machines and mobility allowed sawyers to take their milling equipment from farm to farm, post-and-board (or post-and-plank) fences came into common use. Logs could then be sawed into boards and other construction materials at the farm site. The styles resemble those of rail fences except that square posts and rectangular boards replaced round posts and rails. They are simple, modest, and quite beautiful in open country settings. Boards are sold by the linear foot, according to thickness and width. Both cost and building time are low.

• Protection and security: Moderate. Provides the feeling of protection, but is easy to climb over.

• Visual privacy: Minimal to fair, depending on style.

• Tempering the environment: Closely spaced boards can block drifting snow, but little else.

• Defining space: Good. Attractively marks a simple boundary.

• Finish treatment: Stain, paint, apply clear sealer, or let it weather naturally.

Post-and-Board Variations

Post-and-board fences developed as the products of technological advances, but their horizontal character speaks to their roots as animal enclosures and simple visual boundary markers. Squared posts and boards opened up the chance to employ joinery methods that had been employed in home building and furniture making for centuries. The most immediate effect of this advance was the construction of significantly stronger fences.

Mortised Rail

Mortised rail fences are close cousins of the split-rail fence. The major difference is that they employ mortise-and-tenon joinery to create a very strong and attractive structure. As the boards must be fit into the posts, the fence must be built one section at a time. This is an inexpensive fence to build, but it demands a large amount of labor and fairly advanced woodworking skills.

Ranch Rail

Ranch rail fences require notches (or dadoes) to be cut into the posts, where boards are fitted and nailed. The notches, which can be cut using a circular saw and chisel, create a much stronger fence than if the boards were simply nailed to the face of the post.

Capped Post-and-Rail

Capped post-and-rail fences offer substantially greater privacy and a more contemporary look with a couple of simple style adjustments. The boards can be nailed to the face of the posts, simplifying construction. By closely spacing the boards, you can control the amount of privacy; and by alternating boards of different widths, you can create an interesting design. The cap rail adds strength, both structurally and visually.

Board Fence

Board fences are both common and uncommon: common because there are so many types of them, uncommon because even small variations in the configuration or size of parts will change their appearance remarkably. All the variations illustrated here are common board fences that demonstrate just how uncommon they can be.

Boards can be purchased in standard sizes and shapes at building-supply outlets. The cost varies from moderate to high, depending on the lumber and the style you choose. Construction time also depends on the style, ranging from moderate to high.

•Protection and security: Depending on the height and how close together the boards are placed, the fence can provide a high level of both.

•Visual privacy: Closed styles can provide considerable privacy; more open styles provide less.

•Tempering the environment: The closed surface blocks noise and sun but can force wind into downdrafts.

•Defining space: With closely spaced boards, the fence can define space the way a wall does. Fences can seem overly imposing unless softened by plantings.

•Finish treatment: Stain, paint, or let it weather naturally.

Solid Board

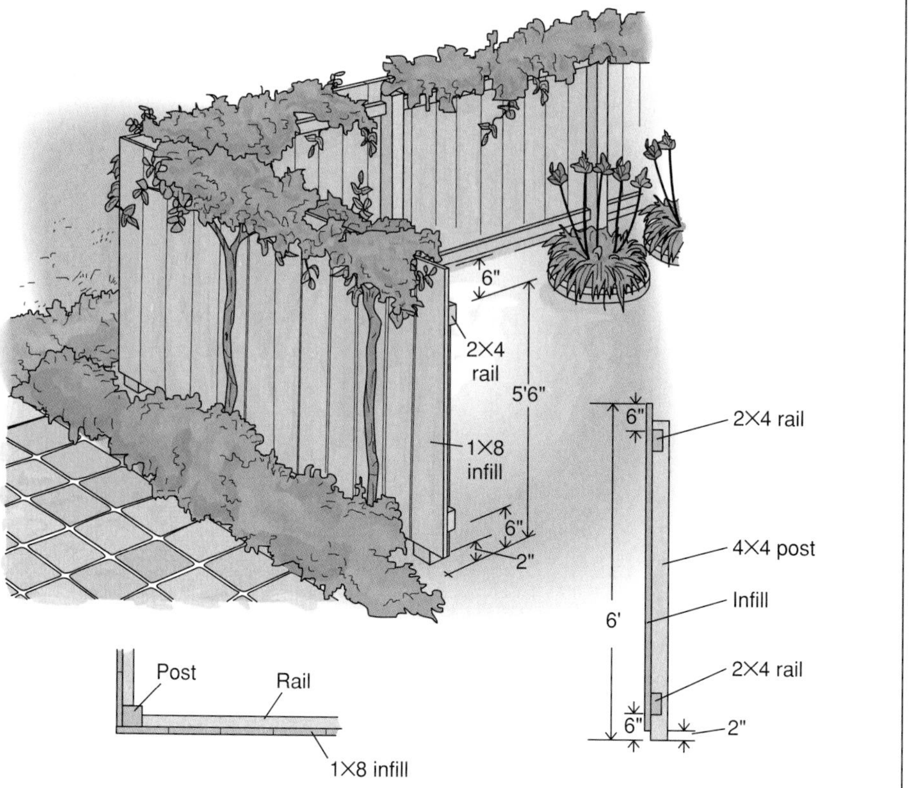

6"
2×4 rail
5'6"
1×8 infill
6"
2"

6"
2×4 rail
4×4 post
Infill
6'
2×4 rail
6"
2"

Post   Rail

1×8 infill

Board Variations

The board fence has a kaleidoscopic character: Tiny changes in its basic design can produce big differences in its appearance. The examples on these pages demonstrate this principle. Building materials remain basically the same, though the way in which they are assembled produces distinctly different styles in terms of board placements (edges can abut, overlap, or have spaces between), board size (boards can be mixed in repeating patterns), and orientation (boards can run diagonally or horizontally).

Solid Board

Solid boards, with no gaps between them, create a wall-like fence that seems to announce Do Not Disturb. The construction is simple (boards are nailed to the rails), the materials uniform, and the cost and time requirements are moderate. The result is a fully enclosed, very private space. This is the basic board-fence design, from which the following variations have evolved.

Boards and Slats

Boards and slats, with gaps between them, compose a fence with a light look and a pleasing visual rhythm. The surface is semiclosed, which yields ample privacy

and an ever-changing play of light and shadow. The widths of the boards, and the amount of space left between them, is a matter of creative choice. It is quick and easy to build and requires a little less material than does the basic board fence. It offers high aesthetic returns in its simplicity, refinement, and appealing proportions.

Featherboard

Featherboard fences are classic, condensed versions of the louver style (see page 28). Boards are mounted between a paired set of horizontal nailers, with each board edge

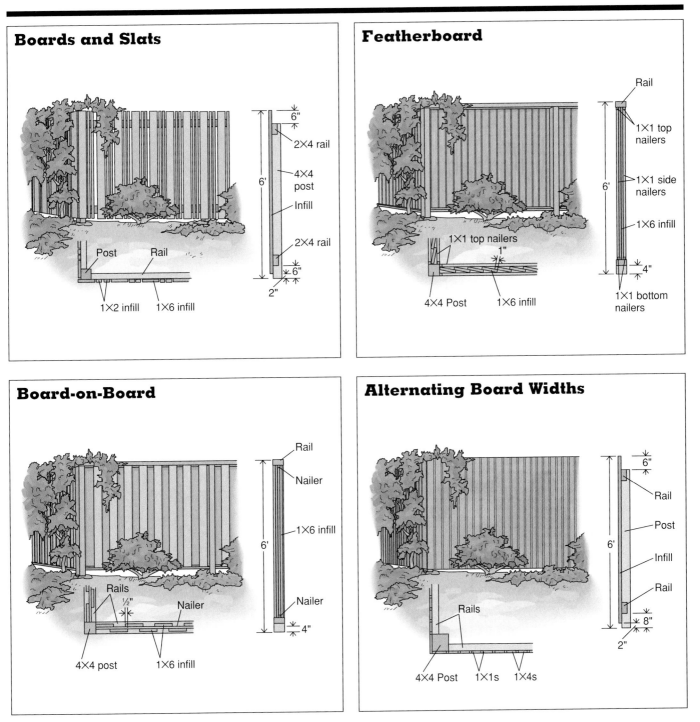

Boards and Slats

6"
2×4 rail
4×4 post
Infill
2×4 rail
6"
6'
2"
Post   Rail
1×2 infill   1×6 infill

Featherboard

Rail
1×1 top nailers
1×1 side nailers
1×6 infill
6'
4"
1×1 bottom nailers
1×1 top nailers   1"
4×4 Post   1×6 infill

Board-on-Board

Rail
Nailer
1×6 infill
6'
Nailer
4"
Rails
½"
Nailer
4×4 post   1×6 infill

Alternating Board Widths

6"
Rail
Post
Infill
Rail
6'
8"
2"
Rails
4×4 Post   1×1s   1×4s

overlapping the next. This produces a fully closed fence for maximum privacy as wall as a pleasant pattern of shadow and highlights. Construction requires a little extra time, since overlapping board edges must be carefully positioned, and the infill is inset to the frame. The cost is about equal to that of the basic board fence.

Board-on-Board
Board-on-board fences give a fully closed fence surface, and, therefore, offer full privacy, but that's not all. Because the boards are fastened to one central nailer but change sides board by board, the configuration allows gentle passage of breezes. The infill is inset to the frame, which requires some care in fitting, but it's worth the effort. The look is clean, slim, and attractively scaled. The cost is about equal to that of the basic board fence.

Board-and-Batten

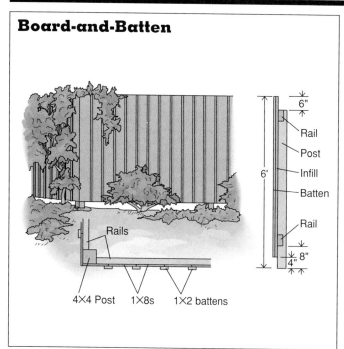

Rail
Post
Infill
Batten
Rail
6"
6'
8"
4"

Rails
4×4 Post   1×8s   1×2 battens

Alternating Bays

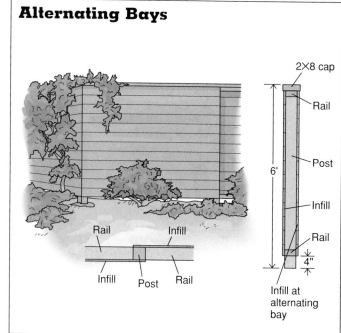

2×8 cap
Rail
Post
6'
Infill
Rail
4"

Rail   Infill
Infill   Post   Rail

Infill at alternating bay

Lap-Joint Grid

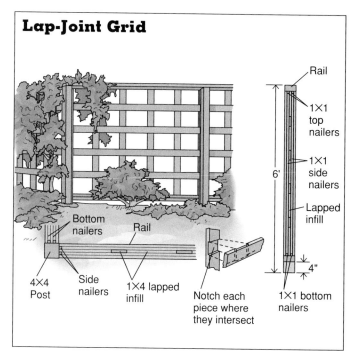

Rail
1×1 top nailers
1×1 side nailers
6'
Lapped infill
4"

Bottom nailers   Rail
4×4 Post   Side nailers   1×4 lapped infill
Notch each piece where they intersect
1×1 bottom nailers

Alternating Board Width

Alternating board width is another way of adding rhythm and scale to a simple, straightforward board fence. The shift from wide to narrow sets a pattern that is distinctive yet calm. Board edges abut, and at each joint, a subtle shadow line is produced, which delicately punctuates the vertical direction. The cost and time requirements are equal to those of the basic board fence, but the visual effect is richer.

Board-and-Batten

Board-and-batten fences achieve a bold textural effect and create a strong, massive feeling with appealing grace. Boards are mounted on the fence framework first, and then battens are fastened to the boards at each joint. Even if the boards shrink as they season, the battens conceal the gaps, so complete privacy is ensured over time. Both construction time and cost are high, but functionally and aesthetically, it may be a worthwhile investment.

Alternating Bays

To have alternating bays is a nice way to share an attractive fence with your neighbor. Here, the boards are fastened to the frame horizontally and bay by bay, and the view changes from a frame exposed to a frame concealed, right on down the line. This variation works as easily with vertically or diagonally mounted infill. You can also alternate the alignment of the boards, from horizontal in one bay, to vertical in the next. Cost and time requirements are the same as those of the basic board fence.

Lap-Joint Grid

Lap-joint grid fences are a pretty way to screen an area without blocking the view. This style invites the eye to rest on the fence and take in the pattern, and then to see beyond to the background. And it works both ways, too—views from the inside out aren't blocked either, but they are screened. You can get a lot of screen for a small amount of material, but construction time is long, since each board intersection requires a pair of notches to create a flush lap joint.

Picket Fence

With irrepressible charm, picket fences have character that has carried them from cottage to village to town to city over many generations. They have a welcoming appearance and a gentle way of marking a boundary, and their traditional style fits well in many different settings.

The fancy cut tops and special finial frills associated with picket fences in the past are now hard to find. Lumberyards still carry pickets and screw-on finials, but only in limited shapes. You can cut your own tops, of course, but that can be quite time-consuming because of the great number of pickets needed to make a fence. Cabinet shops can do special milling and shaping, or the lumberyard may be able to cut the pickets for you for an extra fee. The basic cost of pickets is low, but construction time for the fence is medium to high.

• Protection and security: Will keep children and pets in or out, and pointed pickets can make the fence tricky to hop over.

• Visual privacy: Very little, although pickets tend to capture the eye and hold it.

• Tempering the environment: Will block drifting snow, and close spacing between pickets can soften breezes.

• Defining space: Good. Clearly defines any boundary.

• Finish treatment: Paint generally looks best, especially white, but stain can be effective.

Picket Variations

Pickets offer you a world of variations. Some of the standard ones are shown here, but fancy filigree and other whimsical styles of cutting pickets can delight passersby with their special visual interest. Designing picket tops is a lot of fun, and planning their fabrication is a challenge in ingenuity. Wide-diameter hole saws can easily cut concave curves; a saber or band saw will produce convex curves. To lay out the pickets for shaping, use a hardboard template.

Pickets

Picket Variations

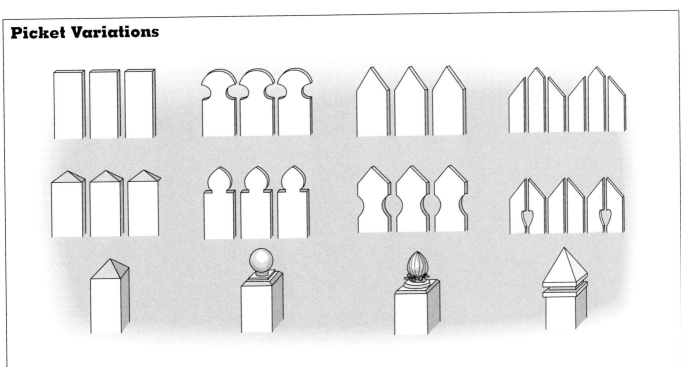

Slats

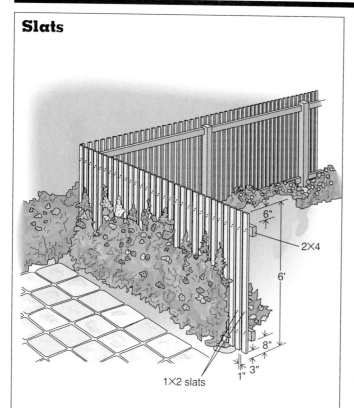

6"
2×4
6'
8"
1"
3"
1×2 slats

Lath

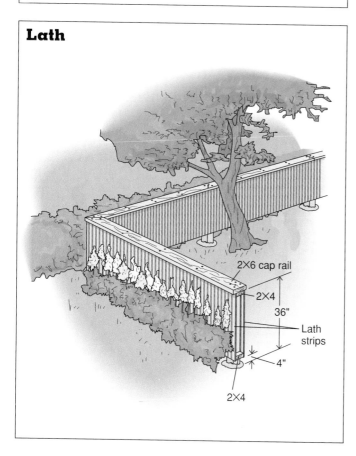

2×6 cap rail
2×4
36"
Lath strips
4"
2×4

Slat Fence

Slats are similar to pickets, but taller. A slat fence has a simple, crisp look and clean lines. The height of the fence and the relatively small scale of the slats give it a feeling of lightness and refinement, suggesting a sophisticated look. It makes an excellent background for a Japanese garden. Slats can be purchased by the piece or by the bundle at lumberyards. Their cost is moderate, though it takes time to assemble a fence of slats. Construction can be tedious.

•Protection and security: Can provide a high level of both, depending on how close together the slats are placed. Similar to that of high board fences.

•Visual privacy: Good. The fence feels open but is hard to see through, although it can magically disappear from view to motorists driving by at certain speeds.

•Tempering the environment: Will block drifting snow and is excellent for softening breezes and filtering light.

•Defining space: Good. Defines space graciously.

•Finish treatment: Paint, stain, or let weather naturally. Dark colors work best.

Lath Fence

A standard lumber material, lath is often used for lattice fences and arbors, but it can also be used vertically as a fencing material. Visually, a lath fence is similar to a slat fence, but shorter. Lath is a very thin material (about ⅜ inch), and, therefore, will not hold up well to rough treatment. (On the other hand, replacing broken lath strips is a simple job.) Lath should not span more than 30 to 36 inches, and it should be firmly attached at both ends. Its rough surface gives it an informal appearance that is naturally at home in the garden. Lath is quite inexpensive. It is commonly sold at building-supply outlets. All the little pieces, however, take time to nail in place.

•Protection and security: Quite good, though it is stronger if the lath is applied to both sides of the fence.

•Visual privacy: Can provide a strong sense of privacy without seeming confining from either side.

•Tempering the environment: Very good for filtering sunlight and softening winds.

•Defining space: Good. Similar to slats.

•Finish treatment: Paint, stain, or let weather naturally.

Stakes

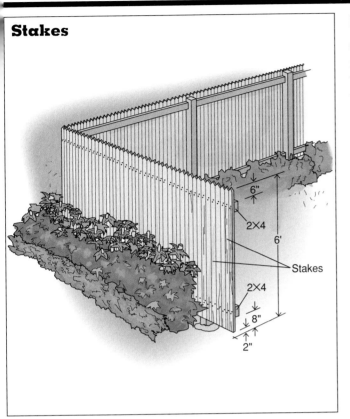

6"
2×4
6'
Stakes
2×4
8"
2"

Palings

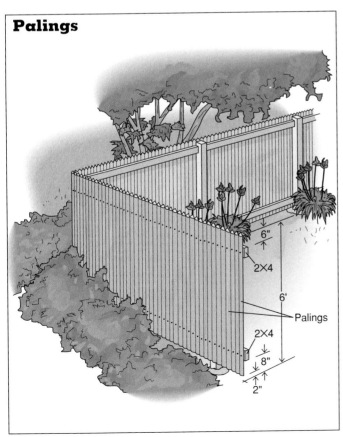

6"
2×4
6'
Palings
2×4
8"
2"

Stake Fence

Split stakes, originally used for supporting plants in vineyards, orchards, and commercial gardens, soon found their way into fences. A handsome, sturdy fence of stakes has a rich surface texture that easily harmonizes with the landscape and garden. Because they are split, stakes are rough, but they have a look that combines orderly refinement and informality. Stakes are sold by the piece or by the bundle at lumberyards. The most durable are redwood and cedar. Their cost is moderate, and building time is just a bit above average.

• Protection and security: Excellent. This is a sturdy, rough-surfaced material.

• Visual privacy: Excellent. The infill is solid.

• Tempering the environment: Blocks noise and provides shade. It may block wind too abruptly, causing downdrafts.

• Defining space: Can be too confining if used around a small area, but very effective when viewed from a distance.

• Finish treatment: Stain or let it weather naturally. Weathered stakes attract moss and lichen easily, adding to their interest.

Paling Fence

Saplings sharpened to a point at the top and split are called palings (or pales). A fence of palings, commonly called a stockade fence, gives the appearance of a dense young forest and works well in a lightly wooded setting. It looks best when left unfinished. Palings may be difficult to find, but lumberyards that specialize in fencing materials may stock them or be able to order them for you. They are expensive, and construction is time-consuming.

• Protection and security: Very good. A paling fence is a scaled-down version of a stockade wall.

• Visual privacy: Excellent. Round poles abut for total privacy.

• Tempering the environment: Blocks wind, snow, and sun, and creates a modest barrier to noise.

• Defining space: Gives such a strong feeling of enclosure that it is best used as perimeter rather than accent fencing.

• Finish treatment: Let weather naturally.

Lattice

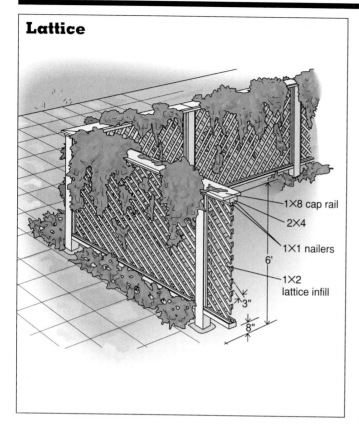

1×8 cap rail

2×4

1×1 nailers

1×2 lattice infill

6'

3"

8"

Louvers

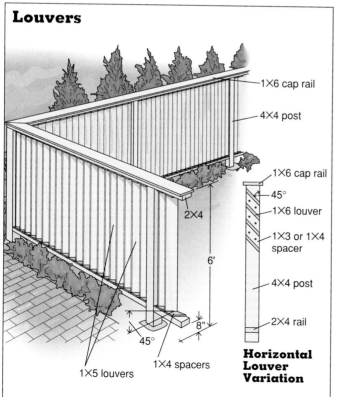

1×6 cap rail

4×4 post

1×6 cap rail

2×4

45°

1×6 louver

1×3 or 1×4 spacer

6'

4×4 post

2×4 rail

8"

45°

1×5 louvers

1×4 spacers

Horizontal Louver Variation

Lattice Fence

A classic in the garden, lattice, with all its crisscross flair, has been used in Persian, Italian, French, and English gardens for centuries. Its formal, regular lines become loose and lively when covered with foliage; light plays across and through the wood.

Lattice allows you to create a particular rhythm and scale by varying the spacing between members. Prefabricated panels are available at building-supply outlets and lumberyards. They are quick and inexpensive to install, and look best inset to the frame.

Lattice panels are available in the traditional diagonal pattern and in an up-and-down grid pattern. Vinyl lattice panels, which are white and do not have to be painted, are also available.

• Protection and security: Good. Provides both in a pleasant, gentle manner.

• Visual privacy: Good. Although not solid, the pattern of the fence, not the view through it, holds the eye.

• Tempering the environment: Softens wind and filters sunlight.

• Defining space: Good. A delightful way to define space and screen an area.

• Finish treatment: Paint, stain, or let weather naturally.

Louvered Fence

A louvered fence has a clean-lined architectural look and a lot of textual interest. Vertical louvers create interesting patterns of light and shadow; horizontal louvers excel at softening and redirecting the wind. Either style is particularly suited to surrounding a patio or swimming pool.

Since louvers are made of boards, any lumberyard can supply the materials. Because the boards are angled, more are required to cover any span. This makes the louvered fence more expensive than other types of board fencing and more time-consuming to build. Horizontal louvers are constructed much like the vertical louvers shown in the drawing, except that 1×3 or 1×4 spacers are attached to the posts, and the 2×4 top rail is eliminated.

• Protection and security: Very good. The fence is sturdy and hard to climb.

• Visual privacy: Moderate (vertical) to good (horizontal).

• Tempering the environment: Softens and redirects winds (especially horizontal louvers); filters and blocks sunlight.

• Defining space: Good for screening, particularly on short runs of two or three sections.

• Finish treatment: Paint, stain, or let weather naturally.

Basket-Weave

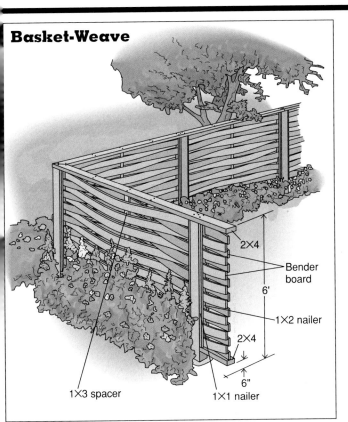

2×4

Bender board

6'

1×2 nailer

2×4

6"

1×3 spacer

1×1 nailer

Plywood

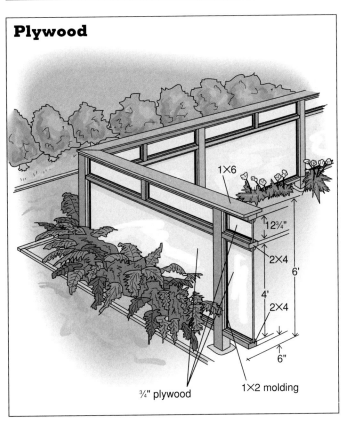

1×6

12¾"

2×4

6'

4'

2×4

6"

¾" plywood

1×2 molding

Basket-Weave Fence

Thin boards, ⅜ to ½ inch thick and 4 to 5 inches wide, are woven together to form a basket-weave fence. The boards are all nailed to the same side of the posts. The woven effect is achieved by placing the centers of the boards on alternate sides of a vertical spacer. These fences look best if the undulation is minimized. This can be accomplished by using only one thin spacer for each bay. Around a small area, basket weave can be somewhat overwhelming. It is fairly easy to install, though it requires patience and dexterity. Very thin materials look best, are surprisingly strong, and are relatively inexpensive. Materials are available at lumberyards.

•Protection and security: Very good. The weave makes a strong surface.

•Visual privacy: Very good. You can't see through it.

•Tempering the environment: Good for softening winds and blocking sunlight.

•Defining space: Can be too dominant for small areas but effective when viewed at a distance.

•Finish treatment: Paint, stain, or let weather naturally.

Plywood Fence

A well-proportioned plywood fence can be an extremely elegant, expansive addition, despite its constructional simplicity. It lends itself to fence designs with 4- and 8-foot modules. Exterior-grade plywood is sold in standard sheet sizes in a range of thicknesses, grades, and surface textures. Some plywood siding has patterns that resemble individual boards. You can also find plywood that has been primed for painting or has been prestained. Choose materials that are thick enough to resist bowing in heavy wind. Plywood is sold at all lumberyards.

•Protection and security: Excellent. Plywood is strong, durable, and difficult to penetrate.

•Visual privacy: Excellent. You can't see through it.

•Tempering the environment: Blocks sun and noise but can cause strong downdrafts.

•Defining space: A very attractive way to define space simply, but it can be overbearing in a small space.

•Finish treatment: Paint or stain.

Clapboard

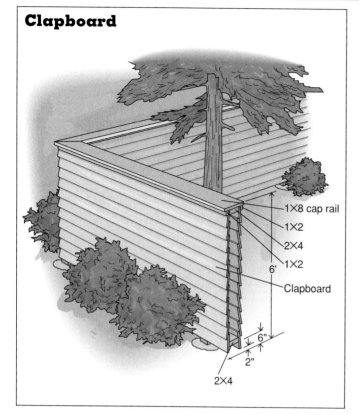

1×8 cap rail
1×2
2×4
1×2
6'
Clapboard
6"
2"
2×4

Tongue-and-Groove

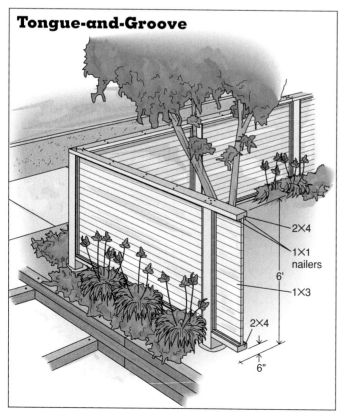

2×4
1×1 nailers
6'
1×3
2×4
6"

Clapboard Fence

Under the right conditions, clapboard can be extremely attractive, especially when it matches your home's siding. The horizontal lines create a wall-like sense of calm and protection. Clapboard gives the fence an architectural quality that ties it to the home more than the garden, but it makes an excellent backdrop for many plants nonetheless. It is best used on level ground or on very gradual, evenly sloping terrain. Clapboard is sold at building-supply outlets. It is not expensive and is fairly easy to install. If boards are applied to both sides of the fence, they enclose a center cavity that is conducive to rot unless it has adequate ventilation and moisture protection along the top.

• Protection and security: Excellent, especially if the fence is high.

• Visual privacy: Excellent. Clapboard creates a solid wall.

• Tempering the environment: Blocks noise, sun, and snow, but can cause downdrafts.

• Defining space: Feels architectural and permanent; might be overbearing in a small space.

• Finish treatment: Paint both sides of the fence and cap off the top for the best appearance.

Tongue-and-Groove Fence

A very solid infill for fencing can be created with tongue-and-groove boards, since their edges interlock. The effect is simple, attractive, and orderly. Tiny shadow lines at the joints give a subtle yet perceptible visual rhythm. Overall, the fence has a refined and elegant look.

This type of lumber is sold at lumberyards and can be expensive. Finger-jointed boards, made from short boards laminated end-to-end, are less expensive but should be painted. Construction time is moderately high, since the boards are inset to the frame and require some fitting.

• Protection and security: Excellent. The material and construction are strong, and the surface is solid.

• Visual privacy: Excellent. The interlocking edges create a solid wall.

• Tempering the environment: Blocks sun; thicker boards may buffer noise.

• Defining space: Good, although solid fencing can be overbearing in a small space.

• Finish treatment: Paint, stain, or apply clear sealer.

Shingles

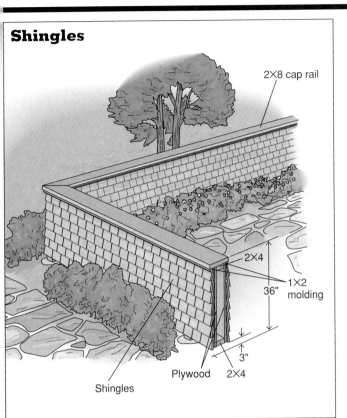

2×8 cap rail

2×4

1×2 molding

36"

3"

Plywood   2×4

Shingles

Wire-Bound Wood Slats

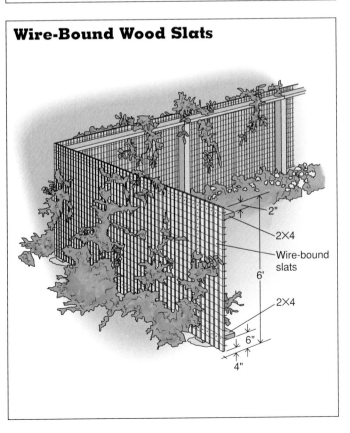

2"

2×4

Wire-bound slats

6'

2×4

6"

4"

Shingle Fence

Providing a highly textured surface, wood shingles give an appearance that is rich, warm, and quite wall-like. If your house is shingled, this kind of fence can unify the site.

Shingles are sold by the bundle at lumberyards and vary in cost according to the grade. No. 3 shingles, which have some knots and are specified for walls, are relatively inexpensive. No. 1 shingles are the most expensive. It takes a lot of time to install shingles, as each one has to be nailed individually. Shingles need to be fastened to a backing surface, such as an existing fence, plywood, or furring strips. They last longer if there is space behind them for air to circulate, drying out trapped moisture.

• Protection and security: Excellent. A shingled fence is much like a wall.

• Visual privacy: Excellent. The taller the fence, the better.

• Tempering the environment: A tall fence can block sun and noise quite effectively. Can cause downdrafts.

• Defining space: Gives a strong feeling of definition and coziness, but can be too confining in a small area.

• Finish treatment: Paint, stain, apply a clear sealer, or let weather naturally.

Wire-Bound Wood-Slat Fence

An excellent temporary solution for a problem spot that requires fencing is provided by wire-bound wood slats. If you choose this kind of fence, staining it dark and covering it with vines will create a pleasing appearance. Time does take its toll on this lightweight material. The fencing is made of regularly spaced slats joined by a wire weft, and you can quickly and easily roll out an expanse of orderly picketlike pieces.

Wire-bound wood slats are commonly sold at lumberyards and home-improvement centers. It is often called snow fencing, since that is its most typical application. It is quite inexpensive and is very easy to install.

• Protection and security: Minimal. Suggests both but is not sturdy.

• Visual privacy: Not much.

• Tempering the environment: Excellent low-cost method for blocking drifting snow.

• Defining space: Good for a temporary situation.

• Finish treatment: Let weather naturally.

Wire-Bound Reeds

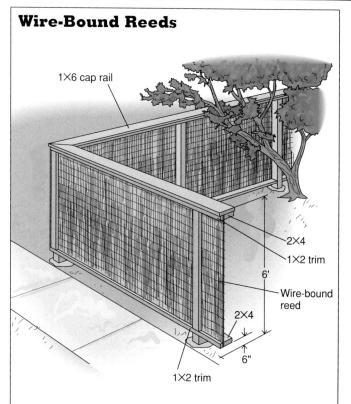

1×6 cap rail

2×4

1×2 trim

6'

Wire-bound reed

2×4

6"

1×2 trim

Bamboo

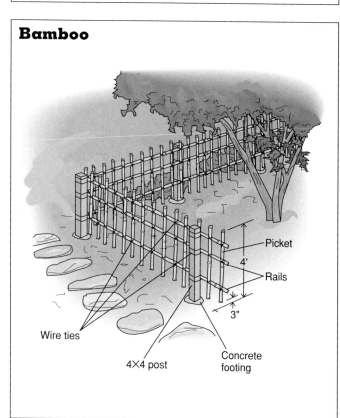

Picket

4'

Rails

3"

Wire ties

4×4 post

Concrete footing

Wire-Bound Reed Fence

Made from freshwater reeds woven every 4 inches with a weft of lightweight, noncorrosive wire, wire-bound reed fencing seems exotic. This fence might look out of place in traditional surroundings. Because the reeds are flexible and easy to break or punch through, durability is not its strong point. This material will last longer if the top and bottom are secured on both sides by wood strips nailed to the rails. Adding an intermediate third rail to the back side of the fence, and stapling the reed fencing to it, will also strengthen the fence.

Some home-improvement centers and building-supply outlets may carry wire-bound reed fencing. It is also available through mail order firms. It is inexpensive and easy to install.

•Protection and security: Suggests both, but it is not sturdy.

•Visual privacy: Good. You can't see through it.

•Tempering the environment: Good for blocking sun and drifting snow. Strong winds could tear it.

•Defining space: Good, but seems temporary compared with most other types of fences.

•Finish treatment: Let weather naturally.

Bamboo Fence

The "four-eyed fence," shown here, is probably the most popular and easily constructed style of fence in Japan. Bamboo is a stiff material, with a warm and soft color. It resists rot quite well, but should be kept away from ground contact. Home-improvement centers and gardening-supply outlets may carry bamboo, but your best source is probably the mail-order firms listed in the "Resource Guide" on page 94. Suppliers can provide you with design and construction details.

•Protection and security: Poor to good, depending on the style and size of bamboo used.

•Visual privacy: Poor to good.

•Tempering the environment: An enclosed style of bamboo fence can soften winds, block snow, and provide shade.

•Defining space: Good. Gives a pleasant, informal feeling of enclosure.

•Finish treatment: Let weather naturally.

Clear Acrylic

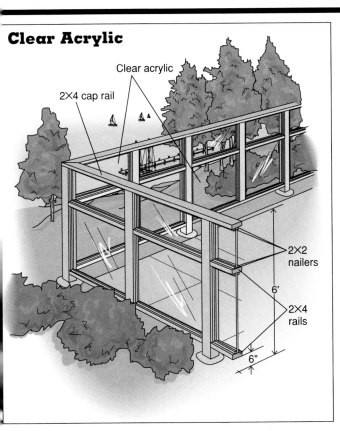

Clear acrylic

2×4 cap rail

2×2 nailers

2×4 rails

6'

6"

Mesh

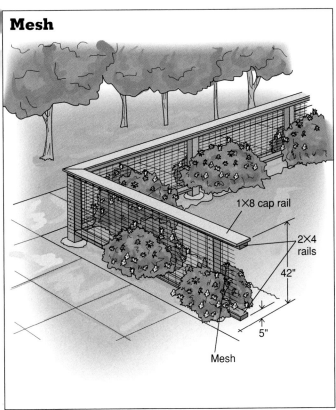

1×8 cap rail

2×4 rails

42"

5"

Mesh

Clear-Acrylic Fence

Not compatible with most natural settings, a clear-acrylic fence would be ideal for some special situations. Because it is transparent, a fence of clear acrylic sheets is ideal when you want to create some security or protection from the wind without losing visibility, for example, around a swimming pool or lake-view property. Acrylic sheets are sold at plastic and building-supply outlets. The cost varies depending on the thickness of the sheet. Polycarbonate, another type of plastic, is stronger than acrylic but can be very expensive. Installation is quick and easy.

•Protection and security: Moderate to good, depending on the strength of the material.

•Visual privacy: By definition, very poor.

•Tempering the environment: Light comes in. Wind goes over the top, but may create downdrafts.

•Defining space: Good at defining space without seeming at all wall-like.

•Finish treatment: Finish only the frame. Paint, stain, apply clear sealer, or let weather naturally.

Mesh Fence

Wire and plastic mesh are available in many identical styles. The mesh is inexpensive, yet can create an attractive fence offering security and protection. The gridlike and rectilinear weaves of mesh are particularly attractive. Heavier wire mesh has intersections or wire welded at the joint, making a rigid joint that looks good for a long time. The plastic coating is usually green or black, and blends well with the landscape.

Wire and plastic mesh can be found at lumberyards, building-supply outlets, and garden centers. The cost is low and the construction time is short. Wire mesh is also available in complete fence, post, and gate systems (in various colors) at a higher cost.

•Protection and security: Good to excellent, depending on material.

•Visual privacy: Very little, unless you train climbing plants on it.

•Tempering the environment: Will block drifting snow but little else.

•Defining space: Defines space in a simple and functional way.

•Finish treatment: None is required.

Chain-link

Chain link

Top rail

Post

4'

Ornamental Metal

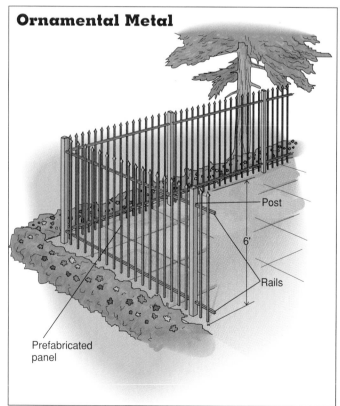

Post

6'

Rails

Prefabricated
panel

Chain-link Fence

Popular for security and low-maintenance reasons, chain-link fencing tends to look stark in garden settings. But special treatments can soften the strident metal look. One treatment is wood insert slats, which are usually stained a redwood color and make a reasonably attractive backdrop for vigorous vines. Another treatment that makes this type of fencing more suitable for gardens is green or black vinyl coating. This fencing is sold at home-improvement centers and building-supply outlets. Installation is only moderately difficult with the right tools.

•Protection and security: Excellent. Chain link was designed for security.

•Visual privacy: Very little. With insert slates or plantings, moderate to good.

•Tempering the environment: Can block drifting snow but little else.

•Defining space: Good, but in a very strict, utilitarian manner.

•Finish treatment: None is required.

Ornamental-Metal Fence

Ornamental forged iron is a classic and durable fencing material. It is still available, but most of today's ornamental metal fencing is fabricated with hollow steel or aluminum tubing. From a distance, the tubular fencing can look identical to forged iron. In the right setting, this type of fencing is pretty and sophisticated. It looks rich, light, and formal and can range from a strongly vertical look to a wildly curving one.

Forged-iron fences and gates are available in a wide variety of traditional styles as well as an unlimited variety of customized styles. Installation can be complex. Contact a local forge or ironworks (or check the "Resource Guide" on page 94) for more details.

Tubular steel and aluminum fences are much easier to install than is forged iron. Installation packages often include fencing sections, posts, flanges, and fittings. You can find these prefabricated products at home-improvement centers and building-supply outlets.

•Protection and security: Very good if the fence is high enough and the infill pattern small enough.

•Visual privacy: Very little.

•Tempering the environment: May block drifting snow.

•Defining space: Good for surrounding a pool or clearly marking a border

•Finish treatment: May require paint.

MAKING A BUILDING PLAN

Regardless of how much they might differ in their appearance and materials, most fences are very much alike. Despite their individual styles, fences are built according to the same construction sequence and are made from similar components. Posts anchor the fence in the earth; rails tie the posts together into a framework; and infill sheathes the frame, forming the fence surface and giving it structural strength.

Choosing a basic fence style entails making decisions about your functional needs and aesthetic preferences. Making a building plan entails deciding how you will actually put the parts together to create the style you choose. Although you are concerned with the entire fence, it is just a series of repeating bays, so you only need to consider the building details for one typical bay.

The fence styles illustrated on pages 20 to 34 provide typical fence designs, detail for detail. If you use one of those designs exactly as shown, skip to pages 43 to 47 to finalize the specifications you'll need for ordering materials and for building the fence. If you'd rather create a custom design, the following discussion focuses on alternative design and construction details. All the options are variations on a basic theme. Some assembly variations actually make building the fence easier; some produce a fence with greater strength; some simply make a prettier fence—and many other variations do all these things at once. Look them over to see which spark your interest or even inspire your own creations.

Design and Construction Variables

Review the following basic design and construction details to see which ones you might choose to incorporate in your own custom fence design to improve its appearance, increase its structural strength, or give it a certain flair.

Shapes and Sizes

Fence materials come in a wide variety of sizes and shapes, which, used in combination, can create a unique visual rhythm and scale. Large structural members look bold and massive and can be softened and tailored by using smaller trim details. Smaller structural members look light and lacy and can be given extra visual weight by

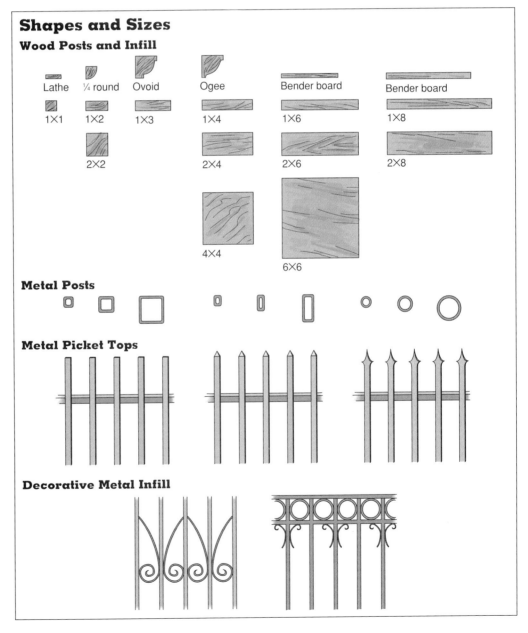

Shapes and Sizes
Wood Posts and Infill

Lathe ¼ round Ovoid Ogee Bender board Bender board

1×1 1×2 1×3 1×4 1×6 1×8

2×2 2×4 2×6 2×8

4×4

6×6

Metal Posts

Metal Picket Tops

Decorative Metal Infill

A Fence Is a Structural System

The accompanying illustration shows the components of a typical fence. It is easy to see the structure that underlies the style. Regardless of how different two styles might look, the structural components remain the same: the footings, the framework, and the infill.

The basic components and their purposes and relationships are discussed below. The pages of other related discussions are also provided. Familiarize yourself with the fence as a structural system, so that when you review the alternative design and construction detail on the following pages, you'll be able to consider their applications in the style you have chosen to build.

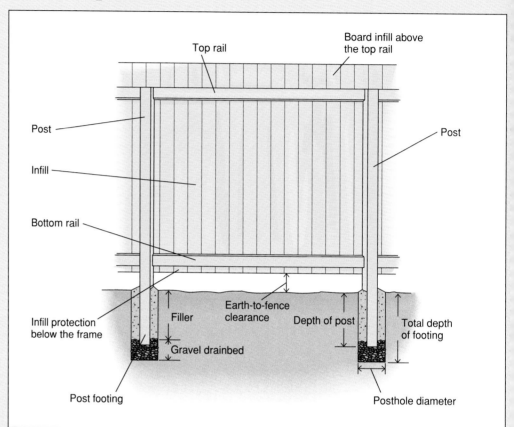

Top rail

Board infill above the top rail

Post

Post

Infill

Bottom rail

Earth-to-fence clearance

Depth of post

Total depth of footing

Infill protection below the frame

Filler

Gravel drainbed

Post footing

Posthole diameter

Footings

The purpose of the footings is to keep the framework upright, stable, and securely rooted in the earth. The footing—no matter what type you choose (see page 45)—consists of the following components:

•Postholes. These should be dug with smooth, straight sides or better yet, with the sides slightly undercut, so the hole is wider at the bottom than at the top. To calibrate posthole diameters and depths, see the table on page 45. For how to dig postholes, see pages 59 and 60.

•Filler. Filler is used to pack the hole and anchor the post to the earth once the post has been positioned and braced. The illustration shows a concrete filler, though an earth-and-gravel mix or just plain earth can also be used to set the posts. See page 62 for filler details.

•Drainbed. The drainbed supports the post and allows rot-promoting groundwater to drain away from its base. Here, a 6-inch gravel bed is used, and the post is embedded 2 inches into it so the concrete can't surround its base. Another way of creating a drainbed is to place a large stone in the bottom of the hole to shield the base of the post from direct contact with earth. See page 60 for further information.

Framework

The framework forms the structure onto which the infill is fastened. Here, the framework shows a typical way of joining posts and rails, but pages 63 to 65 offer attractive alternatives, including special joints and rail-to-post mounting positions. Any type of fence framework consists of the following components:

•Posts. The posts link the fence to the earth. They should be set perfectly plumb and in proper alignment in order to do their job well. Page 44 offers you a summary of alternative post sizes and spacings. Pages 60 to 62 show you how to set the posts.

•Rails. The rails are the cross-members that attach to the posts to form the framework. They need to be cut to fit snugly post to post, and nailed securely in place. Pages 42 and 43 show you alternative ways of mounting rails that negotiate a slope; pages 63 to 65 show you how to fit rails and attach them to the posts.

Infill

The infill forms the actual fence surface. Pages 26 to 34 show you the range of materials and styles to choose from, and illustrate ways that infill can be mounted: nailed to the face of the framework or inset to the frame. Pages 65 and 66 discuss alternative approaches to infill placements, and pages 67 and 68 show you infill installation techniques.

using cap pieces of a slightly larger scale.

Joints

Housed joints, such as mortises, channels, and dadoes, are stronger than others, but they are also more difficult to make. Rails are more typically joined to posts with butt joints. Rails can be installed on flat or on edge, and they can run continuously along the face or top of posts, or butt against each other between posts. Miter joints are often used at corners because they are pleasing to the eye, sufficiently strong, and fairly easy to construct.

Rail Position

Over long spans or under heavy loads, 2×4 rails mounted on flat are much more likely to sag than rails that are mounted on edge. Rails on flat are mounted on their thinner dimension, which is relatively flexible. Rails on edge are stiffer and have less tendency

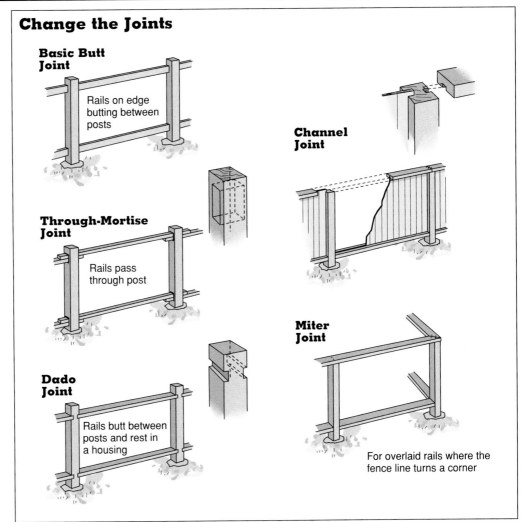

Change the Joints

Basic Butt Joint
Rails on edge butting between posts

Channel Joint

Through-Mortise Joint
Rails pass through post

Dado Joint
Rails butt between posts and rest in a housing

Miter Joint
For overlaid rails where the fence line turns a corner

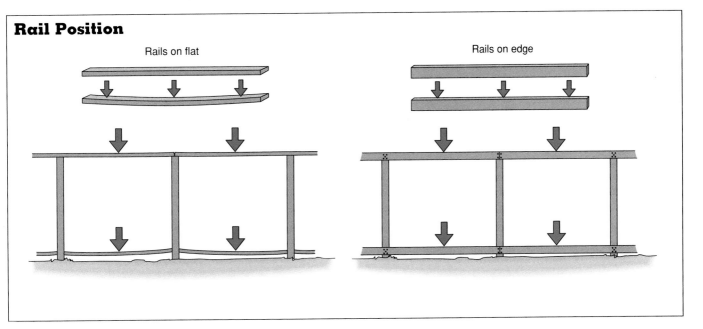

Rail Position

Rails on flat

Rails on edge

Rails on Flat

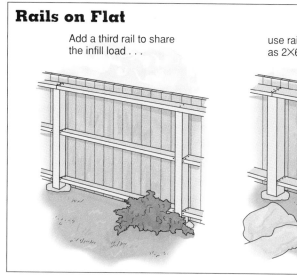

Add a third rail to share the infill load . . .

use rails of a wider dimension, such as 2✕6s with 6✕6 posts . . .

or use rails of a thicker dimension, such as 4✕4s with 4✕4 posts

to sag over longer spans or under heavier loads.

Rails on Flat

If you are using 2✕4 rails on flat over long spans, here are some attractive ways to ensure a stiffer frame, one that isn't likely to sag:

• Add a third rail to share the infill load

• Use wider rails, such as 2✕6s with 6✕6 posts

• Use wider and thicker rails, such as 4✕4s with 4✕4 posts.

Rails on Edge

When rails are mounted on edge, you have a variety of choices for mounting the infill on the frame.

• Attach the infill directly to either side of the rails

• Attach the infill to either side of the rails and cover it with a 1✕4, for a more finished look

• Attach infill members to alternating sides of the rails, so the fence looks the same from both sides

• Cut the infill to fit between the rails, so it rests on

Rail Solutions
Rails Centered on Post

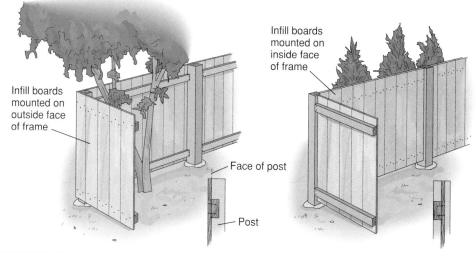

Infill boards mounted on outside face of frame

Infill boards mounted on inside face of frame

Centerline of post

Post

Rails Butted Between Posts Flush With Outside Face

Infill boards mounted on outside face of frame

Infill boards mounted on inside face of frame

Face of post

Post

Rail Solutions

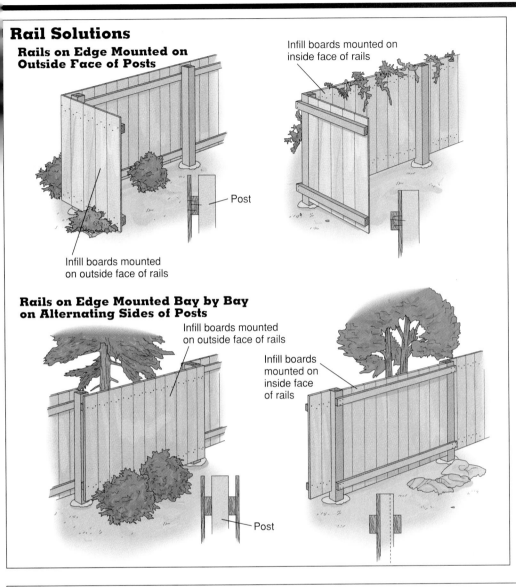

Rails on Edge Mounted on Outside Face of Posts

Infill boards mounted on inside face of rails

Post

Infill boards mounted on outside face of rails

Rails on Edge Mounted Bay by Bay on Alternating Sides of Posts

Infill boards mounted on outside face of rails

Infill boards mounted on inside face of rails

Post

the lower rail and abuts the upper rail.

Fence Tops, Post Tops, and Caps

The details you choose to cap off the fence play an important role. The top of the fence might not be the first thing you look at, but it can be the element that best defines the style. No matter how modest or elaborate, whimsical or simple, top edges are prominent aesthetic elements that attract attention.

There are many ways to cap off your own particular fence design. The boards can be cut in a clean, straight line, or have a special detail cut. The tops can be beveled in succession to form a long, sweeping, concave curve, or they can range in random heights. The boards can sit flush with the top of the rail, or an extrawide trim piece can cap off the edge.

The posts can project above the top rails, with finials pointing skyward down the fence line. Or the posts can

Tops and Caps

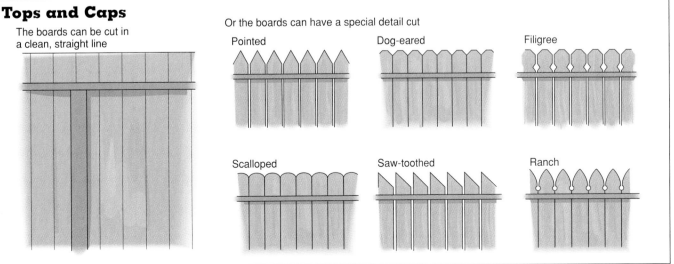

The boards can be cut in a clean, straight line

Or the boards can have a special detail cut

Pointed

Dog-eared

Filigree

Scalloped

Saw-toothed

Ranch

Posts

The posts can reach even higher to support a special border

The border can be open and divided into proportional frames . . .

. . . or it can sport a contrasting infill all its own

The fence can be arbored . . .

. . . or have a linear gable

Tops, Caps, and Posts

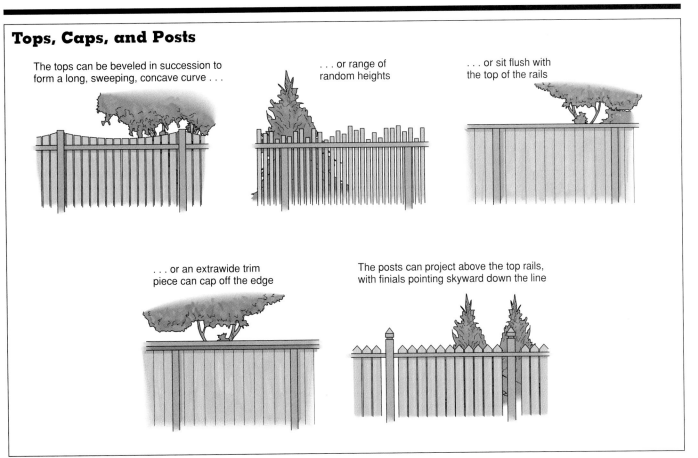

The tops can be beveled in succession to form a long, sweeping, concave curve . . .

. . . or range of random heights

. . . or sit flush with the top of the rails

. . . or an extrawide trim piece can cap off the edge

The posts can project above the top rails, with finials pointing skyward down the line

reach very high to support a special border. The border can be open and divided into proportional frames. Or the border can sport a contrasting infill all its own. The fence can be armored, or it can have a linear gable.

Slopes and Obstructions

Sloped terrain presents a special set of conditions, both when you're planning your fence design and when you're building it. The illustrations on page 42 show you three ways in which the fence can negotiate a change in grade. If you don't know which type of framework will work best for your situation, here's an easy way to find out: Gauge the

slope and plot it out on paper. To experiment with alternatives, sketch them on paper.

How to Gauge a Slope

The purpose of gauging a slope is twofold: It helps you to decide which of three framework approaches you want, and it helps you to determine how much each bay of a stepped frame must project above the one below it.

There are several ways to gauge a slope. The method described here, using an inexpensive line level, is the simplest and will be accurate enough for most situations. Drive two stakes firmly into the ground, one at the top of the slope and one at the bottom (as shown at right). Tie a

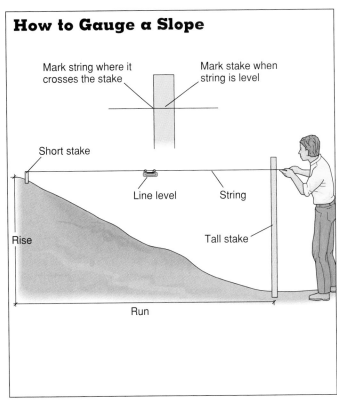

How to Gauge a Slope

Mark string where it crosses the stake

Mark stake when string is level

Short stake

Line level

String

Rise

Tall stake

Run

41

Stepped Framework

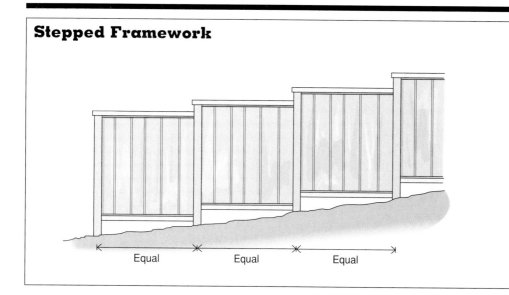

Equal   Equal   Equal

Sloping Framework

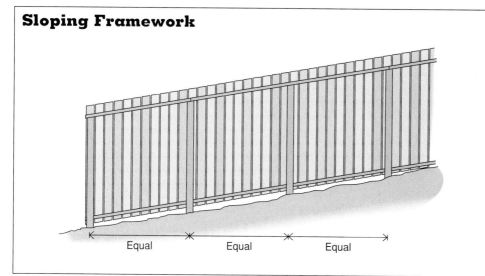

Equal   Equal   Equal

Stepped Framework and Sloping Infill

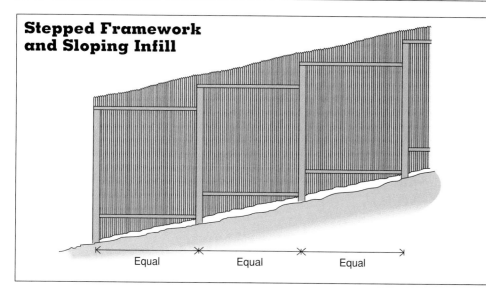

Equal   Equal   Equal

string to the top stake at ground level. Make sure the string doesn't touch anything (cut away some grass, if necessary). Stretch the string tightly between the stakes and level it using the line level, which should be hung at the middle of the string line. (For best results, this should be done when there is little, if any, wind.) When the taut string is level, mark both the string and the stake where they cross. To determine the rise, measure from the mark on the stake to the ground. To determine the run, measure the length of the string from stake to stake. (Note: Leave the stakes in place—they mark the locations of the top and bottom post locations.) Write down both numbers.

Then draw a baseline on graph paper, and plot the numbers to show the slope. Count the number of feet (boxes) of run and mark that. Connect the points, approximating the profile of the slope. Use tracing-paper overlays to experiment with different framework options, and determine a framework approach for your fence.

Stepped Framework

In this approach, the frame itself remains rectilinear and each bay steps up the slope by an equal amount. It works best over gradual, even slopes. Any kind of board infill or sheet material, such as plywood or lattice panels, works well with this type of fence framework. (The sheet material should be mounted inset to the frame rather than overlying it in nail-on style.) The finished effect is crisp, classic, and architectural because the fence remains separate from the earth's slope rather than mirroring it.

To figure out how much each successful bay should step, try this:

1. Count the number of bays in the sloped section. (Your fence-line layout plan should give you this information. See page 16.)

2. Convert the slope's rise into inches; divide that figure by the number of bays. The result tells you the number of inches each bay needs to rise for the fence to step evenly.

Sloping Framework

In this style, each bay is framed to mirror the slope of the earth beneath it. The posts are plumb, but the rails are mounted at an angle so that they parallel the grade. This approach is appropriate for almost any terrain—steep or gradual grades or uneven, rolling terrain. Posts and rails, narrow boards, slats, pickets, stakes, palings, and wire-bound fencing all work well with this type of framework. Although nail-on styles are appropriate, a sloped frame does not lend itself to infill that is inset to the frame.

Stepped Framework and Sloping Infill

This combination solution is often used on very steep grades. Under such conditions it is easier to build a stepped frame, but it leaves large triangular voids along the bottom of the fence and excessively large leaps of graduating rise at the top, which can look awkward and jarring. The solution is to mask them by

Obstructions

extending the infill beyond the frame so that it follows the earth's contour.

Obstructions in the Fence Line

If your proposed fence line crosses paths with tree trunks, rock outcroppings, gullies, or swales, the fence will have to yield the right-of-way. The illustrations here offer a few standard approaches for dealing with such occurrences.

If you are considering nailing the fencing to the trunk of a tree, be aware that you may harm the tree. Puncture wounds subject the living tree to bacterial invasion and generally disturb the flow of life. Even posts placed too close to a tree can destroy its

root system, and the tree can die as a result. Reposition the fence line or stop it short of the tree so the tree can continue to grow.

Plan Completion

Whether you've selected a ready-made fence design from pages 20 to 34 or used one as a basis for your own custom design, there are two tasks to do before your plan is complete. First, choose a footing—the way in which you'll root the fence into the earth (see the illustrated comparison of footing types on page 45 to decide which one will work best for you). The other task is to divide the

fence-line layout plan into bays. If you're using a specified design from the fence-style section, simply follow the guidelines for dividing up the line given on page 46.

If you've developed a custom design, take a look at Post Sizes and Spacing (see page 44) to review your options. If your property slopes, or if there are obstructions in the fence line, the preceding discussion can show you the standard ways in which a fence can negotiate these conditions. Slopes or obstructions probably won't alter your plan, so you can go ahead and complete it. Although when you purchase materials and actually build the fence, these conditions will be treated a little differently.

Post Sizes and Spacing

Post sizes and spacing are both structural and aesthetic issues. The frame itself (posts and rails) creates a visual rhythm. That rhythm can be so pleasing and so much a part of the fence design that what is often considered the back of the fence can easily be more attractive than the front—it all depends on your perspective.

What size and how far apart should the posts be? Keep in mind that visual considerations are subordinate to structural requirements. Your local building code may have strict guidelines that you will be required to follow.

Gate posts, end posts, and corner posts (all of which are called terminal posts) have the heaviest job to do.

Terminal posts should be set deeper (see page 45) and be dimensioned one size larger than intermediate posts. Also, note that the farther apart the posts are, the sturdier the rails must be so they can resist sagging.

4×4 Posts at 6 Feet on Center
This is a tight spacing that bears a heavy infill load well,

looks sturdy, and is nicely proportioned for both tall and low fencing. This spacing carries the eye along the fence at a sprightly pace.

4×4 Posts at 8 Feet on Center
This is the most typical spacing. It works well for lighter-weight infill if the rails are mounted on flat, but is sturdiest if the rails are mounted on edge. (See pages 37 to 39 for alternative rail positions.) This spacing will move the eye down the fence line at a comfortable, gentle pace.

6×6 Posts at 8 Feet on Center
This is a strong spacing, both visually and structurally. The size of the posts is handsomely massive, but the distance between them interjects a pleasing grace. The eye goes down the fence line at a calm pace and enjoys the beauty of the framework.

6×6 Posts at 10 Feet on Center
For members of such large dimensions, 10 feet is an average spacing in terms of strength. But the generous distance between posts gives an expansive quality. Rails should be made of 2×6 stock to bridge the spans with appropriate strength. This spacing moves the eye smoothly down the fence line with a rest in each bay.

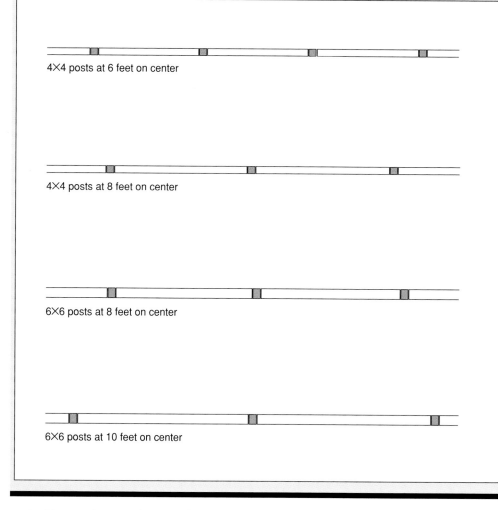

4×4 posts at 6 feet on center

4×4 posts at 8 feet on center

6×6 posts at 8 feet on center

6×6 posts at 10 feet on center

At this stage in your planning, it might be useful to have a look at the chapter on gates (pages 78 to 93). Though you needn't make detailed

decisions about individual gates in order to complete your plan, make sure that the size of gate openings and their placement in the fence line is

just right before you divide the fence line into bays. Look over the following information, then capture your ideas on paper, in every detail.

A sketch of one typical bay gives you the chance to preview the whole, to resolve potential problems, and to

Guidelines for Postholes

These rules of thumb form the basis for a footing design. They are based on average weather conditions and a typical board fence. Local conditions and code may differ; consult your building department and materials supplier for special advice.

Posthole Diameter

The minimum diameter of the posthole depends on which style of footing you are using:

• For earth-and-gravel backfill. The posthole diameter should be at least two times the width of the post. For example: a 4×4 post should have an 8-inch diameter, and a 6×6 post should have a 12-inch diameter.

• For concrete post footings. The posthole diameter should be at least three times the width of the post. For example: a 4×4 post should have a 12-inch diameter, and a 6×6 post should have an 18-inch diameter.

Posthole Depth

The minimum posthole depth is based on the sum of two amounts:

• For intermediate posts. Divide the total height above-ground of the fence (including infill) by 3. To that figure, add 6 inches of depth for the rock or gravel bed.

• For terminal posts. Add 12 inches to the total posthole depth.

Thus, for a 6-foot-high fence, you should dig postholes at least 30 inches deep.

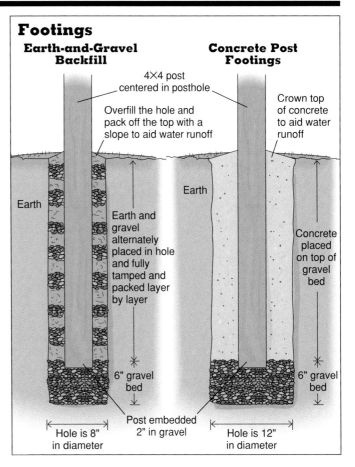

Footings

Earth-and-Gravel Backfill

4×4 post centered in posthole

Overfill the hole and pack off the top with a slope to aid water runoff

Earth

Earth and gravel alternately placed in hole and fully tamped and packed layer by layer

6" gravel bed

Hole is 8" in diameter

Post embedded 2" in gravel

Concrete Post Footings

Crown top of concrete to aid water runoff

Earth

Concrete placed on top of gravel bed

6" gravel bed

Hole is 12" in diameter

confirm the workability of your plan. It also helps you to discover any issues that might require special advice. With the help of your sketch and your fence-line layout plan, your materials supplier can help determine how much material you'll need and will determine the most efficient way to purchase the stock so that waste is minimal.

Selecting a Footing

Each type of footing commonly used in fence construction— earth-and-gravel backfill and concrete-post—works a little differently under certain conditions. The type of soil, the climate, the height and weight of the fence, and the type of post

(terminal or intermediate) will all affect the fence's stability.

Earth-and-gravel backfill has been used for centuries to keep fences of every style upright and firmly planted in the earth. It work best where soils are essentially stable; it tends to lose its grip in soils that slide or crack because of heavy clay content, or in very light soils that cannot resist the lateral loads of wind and weather.

If soil conditions aren't the recommended ones, but the fence is low (or tall and fairly lightweight or open), an earth-and-gravel backfill footing will probably be just fine for intermediate posts. Terminal posts—and especially gate posts—are best set in concrete.

Concrete-post footings are generally recommended for any type of fencing of any height, in any type of soil. They maintain the stability of the fence very well. The footing itself increases the area of the post's bearing surface against the earth, which helps secure and firmly root the fence despite the weather and the wear that it faces. Also, because the post is not in direct contact with the earth, a concrete footing reduces the post's tendency to rot. However, concrete protects the post against rot, provided the bottom of the post is not encased in concrete—but instead embedded 2 inches deep in a 6-inch bed of gravel. This ensures optimum drainage. If concrete caps the bottom of

the post, water will collect there and the post will rot.

Footings and Frost Heave

If you live in a region where frost heave occurs, pay heed to the advice of local experts in the art of fence building. Water expands when it freezes; this causes the earth to heave, which tends to push unanchored posts out of alignment and even out of their holes. In some regions, earth-and-gravel backfill footings are the common choice, since this type of footing keeps water away from the post rather than holding it there. In other regions, builders advocate using concrete post footings for exactly the same reasons. If you're not sure about which type to use, and your local code doesn't specify one, call local materials suppliers or fencing contractors to learn what experience has taught them about the best footing to use under specific conditions.

Dividing the Fence Line Into Bays

The process of dividing the fence line into bays is like marrying an aesthetic point of view to a technical one. When you decided where to put the fence (pages 12 to 16), you may have had a specific post spacing in mind and adhered to it—in which case, simply mark the post locations on your plan. If post spacing wasn't your primary concern, this is how to divide the fence line into bays.

Pick a section of the fence line (from one terminal post to the next) and divide it by the on-center post spacing you want. Do you wind up with a remainder—an odd-sized bay? It's a pretty sure bet that you will, but there are three ways to deal with it. All of them are right, so use the one that works best for you.

•Shorten or lengthen that section of fence line to get rid of the odd-sized bay.

•Split the remainder in half and assign the extra length to the two end bays in that section. The bays will be symmetrically harmonious, even though odd sized.

•Change your post spacing so that each bay in that section absorbs the remainder in equal measure.

Before you decide which solution to use, compute the division for each section of the

Post Spacings

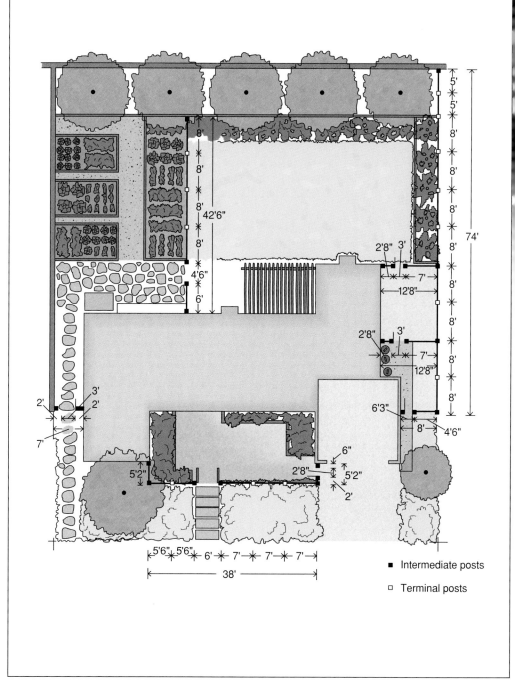

■ Intermediate posts
□ Terminal posts

fence line; you might see a pattern of remainders that will tell you the easiest approach to take. Also, note that different sections of the fence line can have their own post spacings without creating a chaotic

visual effect, as long as the differences between them are subtle. When you've divided the fence line into bays, note the post locations on your plan. Use solid black boxes to indicate intermediate posts,

and open boxes to indicate terminal posts. Write in the dimensions of the bays. This information tells you how many posts you need and the length of each bay. It also provides a layout plan.

Final Fence Design

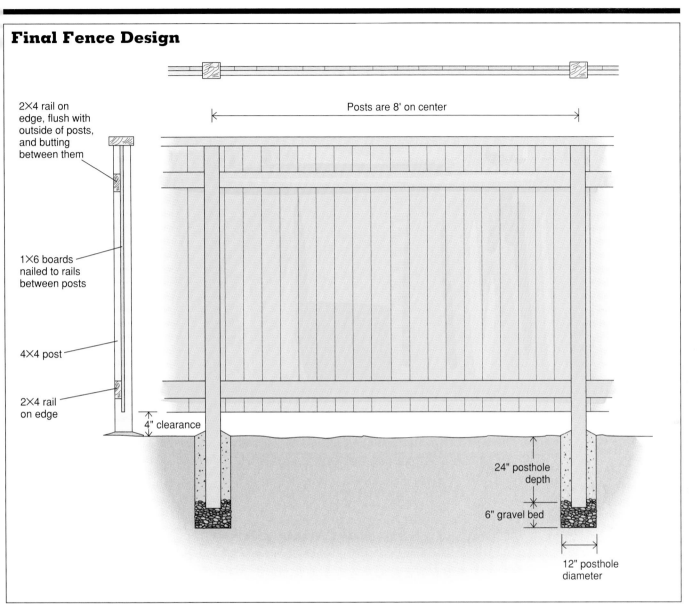

2×4 rail on edge, flush with outside of posts, and butting between them

Posts are 8' on center

1×6 boards nailed to rails between posts

4×4 post

2×4 rail on edge

4" clearance

24" posthole depth

6" gravel bed

12" posthole diameter

A Bay Sketch

Sketching one bay in detail provides you and your supplier with exact dimensions of each component of the fence. Here's how to make the sketch. Tape a piece of tracing paper over a sheet of graph paper, and sketch in a baseline to represent the ground. Plot out the posts, the rails, and the footings; use a scale of 1 inch to 1 foot.

Then tape another sheet of tracing paper over the first one, and sketch in the infill and any special details. This way, if you need to make erasures, the framework remains intact.

When all the parts are in place, trace the information from the bottom sheet onto the top one so that the whole drawing is on the same page. Then assign dimensions to each component of the fence and to the overall height and width of the bay, so that every aspect of the plan is defined, sized, and dimensioned.

Other Drawings

A bay sketch is usually the only drawing you need to order materials and plan construction, but a scale drawing of the complete fence is sometimes useful. If there are obstacles that might interfere with digging postholes, such as rocks or buried pipes, a plan view of the fence will help you plot post locations to avoid them.

A scale drawing of at least three or four bays will also help you verify whether long fence members, such as continuous top rails, can be cut from the lengths of lumber you are ordering. For example, if your bays are 6 feet wide, on center, and you are ordering 12-foot boards to span two bays each, they will not be long enough where one end of the board must cover either post. You will need a 14-foot board. Detailed drawings will help you discover such discrepancies.

BUILDING FENCES

The design phase, for all of its importance, is somewhat abstract. Building, however, is more concrete—both figuratively and literally. The time you take detailing the design of your fence is well spent, of course. The more thoroughly you work out the nuts and bolts on paper, the easier the task of building the fence will be. Still, most people are eager to get started sawing wood and hammering nails.

It is time to assemble the tools, order the supplies, dig some holes, and make sawdust. Any carpentry work requires a sobering dose of caution and common sense. Use your tools properly and safely, respect your neighbors' need for peace and quiet, and don't cut corners to save a little time or money. Most of all, do the best job you can. Try to appreciate the process of creating your fence as much as you will treasure its existence for years to come.

One of the most satisfying phases of fence construction is attaching the fencing to the framework. Here, 1✕8 redwood boards are being nailed to the 2✕4 rails in a board-on-board pattern. Overlapping the boards in this manner allows them to shrink, as they inevitably do, without gaps opening up between them.

GETTING READY

Fence building is a straightforward process that consists of three basic phases: the groundwork, the assembly, and the finish. Each phase uses a different set of skills and tools, some of which you might already have. And those you don't have can be acquired fairly easily.

Planning Ahead

You don't have to do all the work yourself in order to enjoy the satisfaction of having designed and built your fence. Instead, you might like to explore the possibility of contracting out part or all of the installation work.

Before you decide on an approach, consider the project in terms of budget. The dollar outlay for materials is the most tangible form of expense. But your own time and energy are also important parts of the total cost.

How much time do you plan to spend? A week's vacation? A few weekends? Or are after-work hours the only free time you can devote to building the fence?

How skilled are you? Each phase of the work calls for a particular set of skills. Some might be easy for you, but others might be drudgery. It might be worthwhile for you to save your time and energy for the tasks you really enjoy and pay someone else to do those jobs you can't handle.

Building a fence is an excellent project for learning basic carpentry skills, such as layout and framing.

Working With Professionals

First you need to find the names of some reputable contractors. The best way to do this is to solicit recommendations from friends, neighbors, colleagues, relatives, or your building materials supplier. You can also check various forms of advertising (telephone book, classified ads), but it is often true that the best and busiest contractors don't need to buy advertising.

Interview each contractor on your list. Describe the nature and extent of your project—how many postholes need to be dug, for instance, or how many square feet of fence need to be painted. Ask the contractor for references—and check them!

Next, invite bids from those contractors that seem promising. To bid, they will need to visit the site and get a closer look at the details of the project so they can get a firmer idea of cost and scheduling.

If you accept a bid, ask for a contract clearly detailing the work to be done, the time period in which it is to be completed, the quality of materials to be used, and the fee for each phase of the work. The purpose of the contract is to protect both parties; that protection is created by arriving at a shared understanding of the responsibilities of each one. It is a helpful document that frees you both to find satisfaction in the deal.

Phasing the Work

You could turn over to a specialist any one of the three distinct phases of construc-tion—the groundwork, the assembly, and the finish. If you decide to have contractors bid on the job, ask them to itemize their bid according to the following phases and tasks. By comparing the potential costs of the various steps in fence building, you may be able to make a more useful decision on which jobs to do yourself.

The Groundwork

The groundwork consists of staking the layout and marking and digging the postholes. Layout is an easily acquired skill, but it is much easier to do with an additional set of hands. The layout must be done carefully and accurately if the fence is to come out well aligned and true.

If your plan calls for lots of fencing, you will need lots of postholes. How many holes can you dig by hand and still maintain enthusiasm? You can rent a power-driven auger, but keep in mind that it can generate a lot of torque—so much so, in fact, that it can toss you around quite a lot, requiring two strong people to operate it. Bits are available in 8-, 10-, and 12-inch diameters.

You can hire out the work. A posthole-drilling contractor may be willing to stake the layout first, but the other types of firms generally do that as part of the job. If you'd like to have the posts set as well, ask to have that task included as part of the bid.

The Assembly

Assembling the fence consists of setting the posts, installing the fencing, and completing the trim details. The assembly phase requires basic building skills, and a fence project is a good way to develop them. The most exacting step is setting the posts, because it establishes the foundation and framework for the fence. This is much easier to do in teams of two. Each post needs to be plumbed, aligned, and braced. Then, hole after hole, the concrete must be poured, or the earth-and-gravel backfill must be placed and fully tamped. And installing the rails and infill can be fun, fast, and easy. Best of all, you see the product of your efforts take shape before your eyes.

If you're not confident about your ability to measure, cut, and nail with sufficient accuracy, you'll learn how if you do this phase yourself. Should you choose not to do this yourself, consider hiring a landscape or fence contractor, a lumberyard installation service, or a handyperson.

The Finish

Finishing a fence consists of preparing the surfaces and applying the sealer, paint, or stain. Applying surface finishes takes time and skill to do a good job—one that will look attractive and last. Many people find this a pleasant pastime; others consider it a chore. You might find this a relaxing kind of work and quite satisfying for the transformation it brings—the finishing touch. If it's not your preference, a painter can do the job in short order. The finish can be rolled on and brushed out, brushed on, or sprayed on with an airless sprayer on a very still day.

Choosing Lumber

If you have not yet chosen a specific type of lumber for your new fence, selecting it is simply a matter of reviewing the range of options and narrowing your selection down to one or two. That seems easy enough (and it is), but the range can be wide, and there are several approaches you might take.

Your options largely depend on what is locally sold and available. Lumber is somewhat regionally specific in that it is shipped to locations where it will sell and where market demand is closely tied to local building traditions. The materials and techniques used for construction in your area have earned their popularity by trial and error over time; they can be trusted to work. But your choice needn't be limited to these traditions if other types of materials or techniques seem better to you.

Consider carefully the following characteristics when choosing building materials for your fence:
- Availability
- Performance
- Longevity
- Durability
- Cost
- Appearance: grain pattern, surface texture, natural color
- Finish possibilities
- Workability
- Climate
- Toxicity

Some of these considerations will be important to you; others won't. Cost, appearance, and performance are generally the most prevalent

Pressure-Treated Lumber

The most widely available type of pressure-treated lumber is southern yellow pine that has been treated with CCA (chromated copper arsenate). It is easily identifiable by its green tinge. ACA (ammoniacal copper arsenate) is a preservative developed to treat Douglas fir and other hard-to-treat species of wood. This form of treatment can usually be identified by cuts in the surface of the lumber, made to improve penetration. ACQ (ammoniacal copper quaternary ammonia) is a newer preservative. It contains no ingredients classified as hazardous.

When it is properly treated and handled, pressure-treated lumber poses little, if any, health or safety risk. The preservative agent binds with the wood fibers, minimizing the chance of leaching into the soil. Still, the Environmental Protection Agency classifies arsenic and chromium as hazardous substances, and manufacturers recommend that you follow certain precautions when handling treated wood:
- Always wear gloves.
- Don't inhale the sawdust when cutting or sanding; wear a dust mask.
- Don't burn the scraps, especially in a woodstove. Dispose of them with ordinary trash.
- After handling, wash hands before eating or smoking.
- Launder clothing separately that has contacted treated wood or sawdust.

Pressure-treated lumber is sold in different *retention levels*—a measure of how much preservative the lumber holds. Posts and any other pieces that are in ground contact or that are likely to stay wet should have a retention level of 0.40. Other fence components, such as pickets and infill, can be built with lumber treated to 0.25.

Pressure treatment is not a substitute for finishing the wood. A couple of weeks after construction, apply water-repellent sealer, with several coats on cut ends. Then, after it has dried for two to three months, apply paint or stain. The wood will need to be refinished from time to time. An unfinished fence built with treated wood will gradually turn to a pleasant, weathered gray, but it may not last nearly as long.

concerns, though you'll decide which matter most to you.

You'll want to find the best-quality material within your budget. A simple fence can require a sizable expenditure, though careful shopping and negotiating can be worth the effort. The information here can help you compare differences in cost for the kind of fence you're planning.

If you want to match your home's exterior, an existing fence, or some other outdoor construction in color, texture, and grain, your options are narrowed considerably. If your design calls for a particular surface finish, make sure the lumber is compatible with it.

Wood Decay

Wood materials are subject to decay—it is a fact of nature. And yet some species contain heartwood that is naturally able to resist decay and insects. Redwood, red cedar, and black locust are perhaps the most commonly milled woods in this rot-resistant category. The heartwood sections of these trees are naturally saturated with resins that make the wood fibers useless as food for fungi and termites.

Because of their workability, appreciable beauty, longevity, and relative scarcity, these species are more costly than other softwood species that are good building products but offer no natural resistance to decay.

Pressure-treated lumber is a product that has undergone a process to simulate this natural state of decay resistance by forcing preservatives deep into the wood fibers. Some common inexpensive softwood species (pine, hemlock, spruce, fir) are rendered decay-resistant in this way. Pressure-treated lumber is readily available in a variety of sizes, can be painted or stained, and can last a long time. (See Pressure-Treated Lumber on page 51.)

Why would you want to choose a more expensive material for outdoor construction when the less expensive materials have similar merits? There are many reasons: in order to match the new fence to existing outdoor building materials; out of a preference for the grain patterns, texture, weathering or finishing qualities; because of concerns about toxins leaching into the earth; local availability; or a regard for tradition. Some of these reasons may apply to your situation.

Species and treatments aside, there is also the issue of climate.

Some regions have such dry climates that virtually any softwood, decay-resistant or not, can be used for outdoor construction with little likelihood of rot. Other regions are so humid and wet that the processes of deterioration are accelerated.

Plywood

Plywood is produced in a variety of sizes, thicknesses, textures, species, and grades. Any plywood used for outdoor construction must be an exterior-grade material—fabricated with glues that will not deteriorate when exposed to moisture—so that the sheet will stay flat and veneers will stay tightly bonded.

Use AA exterior grades for sheathing that will be stained or painted or seen from both sides. Any surface defects will show through the finish and detract from the appearance. A lesser grade will be just fine for sheathing that will be covered with some other material, such as shingles.

Remember that fences take a lot of wear and tear from the elements. Wind in particular puts a lateral load on both the framework and the infill. Plywood is stiff and rigid; the thicker the material, the greater its rigidity, which keeps the fence

Prefabricated Fence Bays

Building-supply outlets and fence dealers often carry prefabricated wood-fence bays, or panels. If you want to put your fence up in a hurry, these products may be worth considering. The bays are typically sold in 6- and 8-foot lengths, leaving you with the task of simply installing posts, nailing on the bays, then applying the finish. You may even discover that it is less expensive to buy prefabricated bays than to build your own.

Before you decide to build with prefabricated bays, however, examine them carefully. They are available in a wide variety of styles, prices, and grades. You may find that lower cost means short- cuts in quality of materials and construction.

Keep in mind the following questions as you consider your options: From what kind of wood are the fences built? Are the rails made with 2✕4s, or much weaker 1✕3s or 1✕4s? Is the wood pressure treated or untreated? Is the infill attached with nails or staples? Are the fasteners hot-dipped galvanized? Finally, can you find a style that you like?

Read the sections of this book on design and construction before you buy prefabricated bays. That way you will be better equipped to judge whether the product is a worthwhile investment.

looking flat, smooth, and crisply architectural.

Look Before Buying

The best way to get a sense of which materials are right for your fence project is to take an exploratory trip to the lumberyard.

Look at the different species and examine their color and grain patterns. Assess quality differences between the grades. Note how rough-sawn material differs in appearance and size from surfaced lumber.

Compare pressure-treated with untreated products.

If you don't have a good idea of what you'd like to use, take your fence-line layout and elevation sketch with you and ask a salesperson to give you appropriate recommendations and an idea of costs. Then take a second look. Go through the lumber racks and check for defects. Sight down the length of boards on both the flat side and the edge. Are they crooked? Warped? Or square and flat? Check for knots. Are they small or tight? Loose and large? Look for checks and splits. If the wood hasn't been kiln dried, you can expect that more checks and splits will develop as the lumber seasons.

When you have the issues sorted out and have a good idea of the material you want to use, shop around to get a comparison of materials and costs. You might find that a higher-grade material costs less at one yard than does a lower grade material at another yard.

Nominal Versus Actual Dimensions

The dimensions used to describe a piece of lumber—1×4, 2×4, 2×6, and so forth—are its nominal dimensions: the size of the board before surfacing. For example, the actual size of a surfaced 1×4 is ¾ inch by 3½ inches; a 2×4 measures 1½ inches by 3½ inches; and so on.

Reductions in size from nominal dimensions to actual ones are generally consistent, although pressure-treated boards may vary slightly from untreated boards. If size is particularly significant to your design, you might want to measure actual board dimensions. For example, if you have planned a rough-sawn 1×6 board infill, with spaces between, to be inset to the frame, you'll want to know exactly how many boards and the size of the spaces it would take to actually complete a bay.

Fasteners and Connectors

You'll need to select the right size and type of fasteners and connectors for your project. For most fences, nails are the simplest and least expensive fastening options. Screws and bolts cost more and take longer to install, but they are a good choice if you want to create a stronger connection.

The type of metal used to fabricate a particular nail is an important consideration. Some nails rust readily, and others won't ever rust. Those that do

rust will leave dark stains on the fence surface, produce rust stains that bleed through a coat of paint, and generally weaken the nail's ability to function, which ultimately weakens the entire fence.

Hot-dipped galvanized nails resist rust much better than do regular steel nails. Aluminum nails are better at resisting rust, although they aren't quite as strong. They are a good choice for a painted fence. Stainless steel nails are best against rust, especially near saltwater, but they can be very expensive and difficult to find. Ring-shank and twisted-shank nails hold better than smooth (common or box) nails

do, but they are harder to remove. Bolts, nuts, and washers should be hot-dipped galvanized, and screws should be galvanized or stainless steel.

Although a particular style of infill might require special nail sizes and shapes, for most fence projects, the nails listed below will do well.

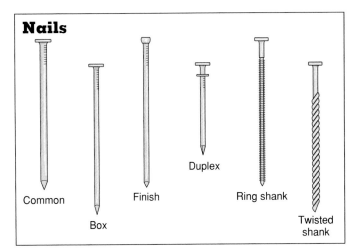

Nails

Common

Box

Finish

Duplex

Ring shank

Twisted shank

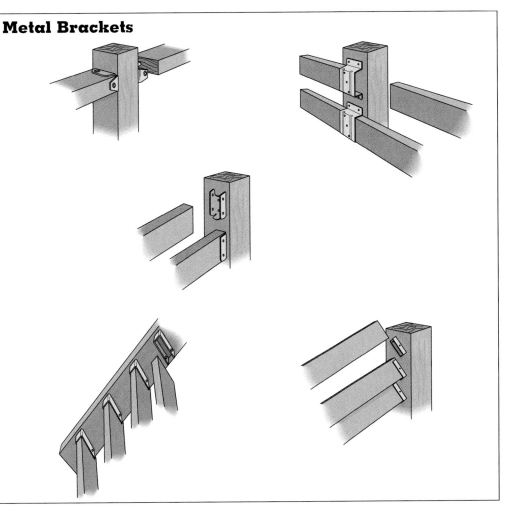

Metal Brackets

- •Common nails for the frame—2-by stock or thicker (16d)
- •Box nails for the infill—1-by stock or thinner (8d or 10d)
- •Finish nails for the fine trim details (6d or 8d)
- •Duplex nails come in handy during installation as temporary fasteners. They have a double head, which makes them easy to pull out when you strip away braces, for example.

Metal fence brackets can be a smart choice for quick installations and solid connections. Brackets can be used to join rails to posts, prefabricated fence bays to posts, and louvered boards to posts (horizontal louvers) or rails (vertical louvers).

Estimating Costs and Preparing Materials

If you'd like to estimate your materials costs at home, you'll need some current price books or the names of a few materials suppliers. It should take only a couple of hours to figure it out from scratch.

On the other hand, if you'd like to get a quick idea of what the costs might be, here's an easy way to do it. Call a lumberyard and ask a salesperson to give you the materials cost for the basic style of fence you're planning to install. You'll need to provide basic information similar to the example below:

- •Fence style: Nail-on board fence with a 1×6 board infill.
- •Width and height of the bay: Posts are 7 feet on center;

each bay has two rails; the fence is 6 feet tall.

- •Species of wood: First choice: surfaced cedar; second choice: pressure-treated southern yellow pine.
- •Type of footing: Concrete post footings with posts set 30 inches deep.
- •Finish treatment: None; it will weather naturally.

The salesperson can probably compute the cost for you right there in a rough estimate form, or return your call later with the answer. Don't hesitate to ask for this computation from several suppliers. That way, you will be able to compare costs as well as service, both of which can be important in any construction project.

Your Lumber Order

To place an order, you'll need to specify exactly the material you want—its classification and category. Besides giving the species and grades, you'll have to specify the material dimensions—the thickness, width, and length of each of the components. For example, *2×4 by 16 feet* might describe the dimensions of a rail that spans three posts.

When you place a lumber order, be prepared to specify the following:

- •Species: The natural characteristics of strength, color, grain pattern, weathering traits, finish, and ability to resist decay will vary with each species.
- •Grade: The type and number of defects (knots, checks, etc.) that you can expect to encounter. These defects affect the material's performance

Materials Needed to Set the Posts

The amount of material you need to set the posts depends on the total number of posts, the diameter and depth of the postholes, and the size of the posts. To arrive at an estimate, you will need to work a bit of math. Use the following examples as a guide. Keep these formulas in mind for estimating volumes:

1 cubic yard = 27 cubic feet

1 cubic foot = 1,728 cubic inches

For cylinders: volume = π [3.14] $\times$ radius squared $\times$ height

For posts: volume = height $\times$ width $\times$ length

To determine how much backfill or concrete you will need for each posthole, calculate the total volume in the posthole (excluding the gravel bed) and then subtract the volume that the post will fill.

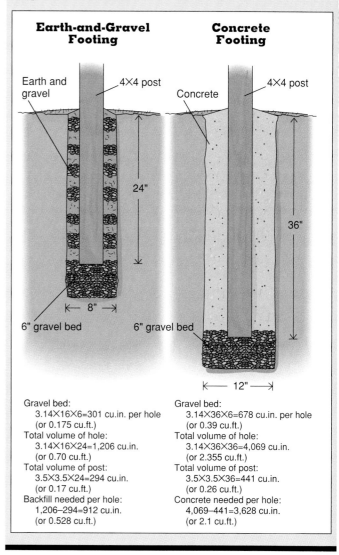

Earth-and-Gravel Footing

Earth and gravel — 4×4 post — 24" — 8" — 6" gravel bed

Concrete Footing

Concrete — 4×4 post — 36" — 12" — 6" gravel bed

Gravel bed:
3.14×16×6=301 cu.in. per hole
(or 0.175 cu.ft.)
Total volume of hole:
3.14×16×24=1,206 cu.in.
(or 0.70 cu.ft.)
Total volume of post:
3.5×3.5×24=294 cu.in.
(or 0.17 cu.ft.)
Backfill needed per hole:
1,206−294=912 cu.in.
(or 0.528 cu.ft.)

Gravel bed:
3.14×36×6=678 cu.in. per hole
(or 0.39 cu.ft.)
Total volume of hole:
3.14×36×36=4,069 cu.in.
(or 2.355 cu.ft.)
Total volume of post:
3.5×3.5×36=441 cu.in.
(or 0.26 cu.ft.)
Concrete needed per hole:
4,069−441=3,628 cu.in.
(or 2.1 cu.ft.)

Preinstallation Prep Work

Depending on the type of finish treatment you're planning, you might choose to do the prep work before you install the fence. Since you can prepare most of the materials all at once before they're assembled, these steps are faster and easier at this stage.

Applying Water-Repellent Sealers

Stack 4✕4s together to form a trough large enough to hold the longest pieces of material. Line the trough with a couple of full-size thicknesses of heavy-duty plastic sheeting (make sure it has no tears in it). Fill the trough with the sealer and put all materials through the bath. Lean them against a wall on end to dry, or carefully stack them log-cabin style.

Applying Primer, Paint, and Stain

Set out a pair of sawhorses on a piece of plastic sheeting, then lay a batch of lumber down on them. Roll on a coat of primer, paint, or stain over exposed surfaces. When they're dry, flip the batch over and do the other side and the edges until all the surfaces are coated. Let them dry in place or carefully lean the batch up against a wall to dry.

and cost. Grading systems vary for different species.

• Appearance: The type of milling treatments the material has had: rough-sawn, surfaced smooth, or hand-split.

• Seasoning: How green is the wood—how much has it dried, and, therefore, how much can it be expected to shrink or change shape as it dries.

• Dimensions: Provide these in this order: thickness, width, and length.

You will probably find that you can negotiate a better price for materials if you place the full order with one lumberyard. You might like to have the load delivered, as well. This approach can save you time and money.

Storage and Handling

Before installation, lumber should be protected from exposure to direct sunlight and moisture. If the lumber has not been kiln dried, it is likely to have a high moisture content and should be allowed to dry for several weeks before you begin building your fence.

Stack the boards so that they are flat and evenly weighted with spacers (stickers) between them. Store under cover or in shade.

Kiln-dried lumber should be dry enough to build with right away, but it should also be protected from rain and direct sunlight prior to construction.

BUILDING THE FENCE

The plans are all drawn, the materials have been delivered, and the tools gathered. If you have taken your time preparing for the construction phase, you'll quickly learn that it was time well spent.

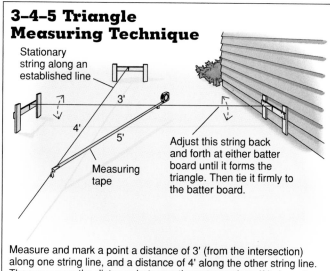

3–4–5 Triangle Measuring Technique

Stationary string along an established line

3'

4'

5'

Measuring tape

Adjust this string back and forth at either batter board until it forms the triangle. Then tie it firmly to the batter board.

Measure and mark a point a distance of 3' (from the intersection) along one string line, and a distance of 4' along the other string line. Then measure the distance between those two points. If it doesn't exactly equal 5', adjust the string lines until it does. The angle is then a perfect 90°. A framing square can also give you a quick check.

Building a fence is a lot like cooking—if the recipe is wrong, or overly complicated, the whole process will suffer, and the end result will be less than satisfactory. So, before you begin digging holes and hammering nails, check your plans one more time. With that extra measure of reassurance, you'll be able to proceed more efficiently and focus your energy where it should be now—on building.

Staking the Layout

Installation begins with staking the layout, the point at which your plans leave the paper and get down to earth. It consists of two phases. First, you will install a pair of batter boards for each section of the fence line (see facing page). Second, you will stretch taut a string line between each pair of batter boards and check their positions; then adjust them accordingly.

As you stake the layout, remember that no part of your fence, including the concrete footings, should cross property lines unless you have a written agreement with your neighbors. As a matter of course, fence builders often stake out the fence line so that it falls at least 6 inches inside the legal boundaries, just to be on the safe side.

During the layout stage, the string lines indicate the exact fence centerline (along its length). Later, when you're setting and aligning the posts, you will reposition the string lines to indicate the outside surface of the fence. But for now, you want to make sure that they are exactly where you want them to be—each section forming the desired angle with the adjacent section.

Tools and Supplies

Look over the illustration and text to familiarize yourself with the basic procedures. Then use this list to make sure you have the tools and supplies you'll need:

• Mason's twine (it doesn't break when stretched taut)
• Stakes and 1×3s for batter boards
• Box nails
• Hammer
• Sledgehammer
• Measuring tape (50 or 100 feet)
• Framing square

The Steps of Layout

Here are the steps required for layout:

1. Install the batter boards. Drive a pair of stakes (about 18 inches apart) securely into the earth 2 to 4 feet beyond the end point of each section of fence line. (Use your fence-line layout plan as a reference; see page 16.) If the fence will abut an existing house wall or fence, drive the stakes in just in front of it.

2. Nail a length of 1×3 across the outside faces of the stakes, using two nails per stake. See the detail of a batter board below.

3. Stretch a string line between each pair of batter boards. Make sure it's taut, as this is the only way it can indicate a perfectly straight line. If the distance between batter boards is so long that the string won't stay taut, add a third batter board at midspan, and tie a separate line taut between each pair. (See the note at the end of this list.)

4. Adjust the string lines. Move the string lines along the batter boards to adjust their positions. Double-check to be sure that their placement reflects the positions you had in mind when you made the design. For instance, if a section of fence was planned to parallel a terrace or the wall of a house, measure from those existing site features to see if the line is properly placed. Adjust it accordingly. Where two sections of fence line abut, or where a section terminates against an existing wall, carefully check their intersection to make certain they're correctly angled to each other. For right angles, use the 3–4–5 triangle measuring technique illustrated above. (For other angles, a simple sight check will probably be enough.)

Note: If bushes or other obstructions impinge on the string line between the batter boards, you won't get the accurate reading you need. If the impingement can be removed, propped out of the way, or trimmed back, do so. If it's a permanent part of the landscape, such as a rock outcropping that the fence will have to go around, lengthen the batter-board stakes so that the string line clears it. Where level earth begins to slope, establish a batter board at the

A Sample Fence Line Layout

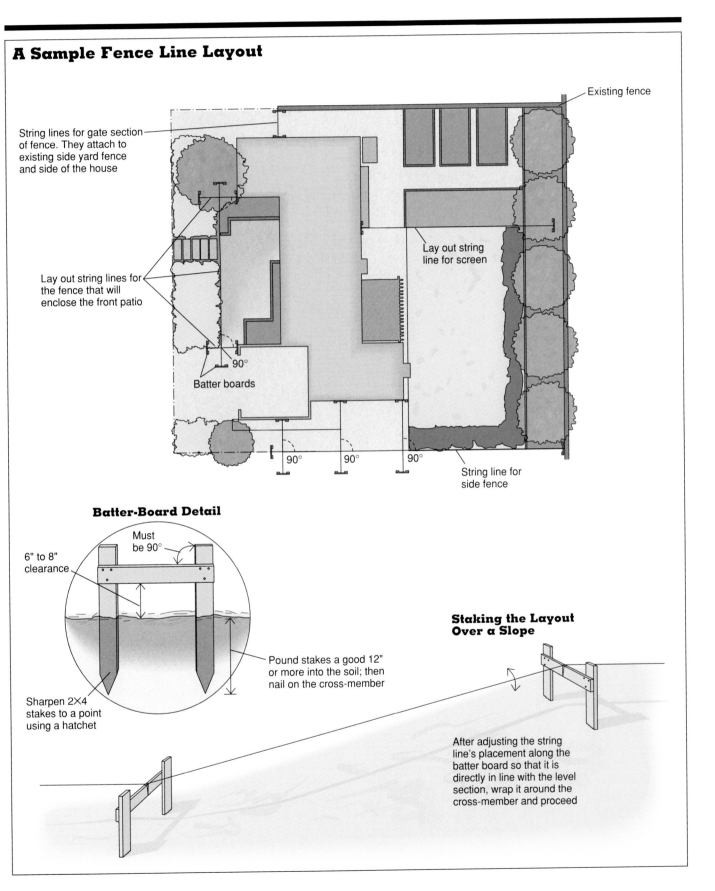

Existing fence

String lines for gate section of fence. They attach to existing side yard fence and side of the house

Lay out string line for screen

Lay out string lines for the fence that will enclose the front patio

90°

Batter boards

90°   90°   90°

String line for side fence

Batter-Board Detail

Must be 90°

6" to 8" clearance

Pound stakes a good 12" or more into the soil; then nail on the cross-member

Sharpen 2×4 stakes to a point using a hatchet

Staking the Layout Over a Slope

After adjusting the string line's placement along the batter board so that it is directly in line with the level section, wrap it around the cross-member and proceed

Flagging Posthole Locations

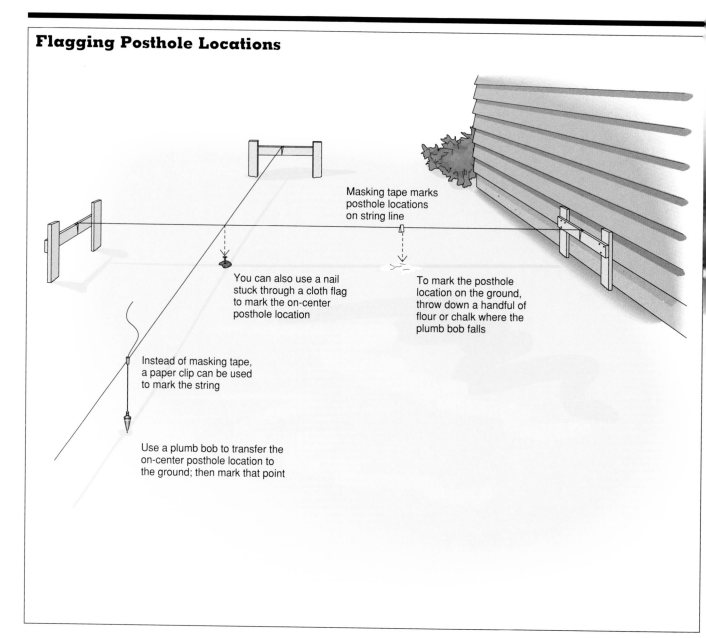

Masking tape marks posthole locations on string line

You can also use a nail stuck through a cloth flag to mark the on-center posthole location

To mark the posthole location on the ground, throw down a handful of flour or chalk where the plumb bob falls

Instead of masking tape, a paper clip can be used to mark the string

Use a plumb bob to transfer the on-center posthole location to the ground; then mark that point

break and continue the line from there. At these points, you'll have to sight down the line from the top of the slope to be sure it hasn't inadvertently been skewed off the centerline you've just established over level ground. When everything is placed just as you'd like it to be, you're ready to mark out the posthole locations.

Marking the Postholes

Accurately marked posthole positions not only ensure a pleasing visual rhythm in the finished fence, they also make it a lot easier to build—minimizing the need to do special measuring and cutting to fit.

Marking posthole locations consists of two phases. First, measure and mark the string line where posts will be placed; mark and flag those locations on the ground. Then dig the holes at the flagged locations.

Use the fence-line layout plan as a reference. Don't be discouraged if you have to adjust your plans a bit. As they take shape in three-dimensional form, they can change a little, sometimes even a lot. You may want to adjust the post spacing accord-ingly (see pages 46 and 47 for how to divide the fence line into bays).

You will need the following tools and supplies for marking the posthole locations:
- Measuring tape
- Plumb bob
- Masking tape
- Cloth scraps and long nails, or a can of spray paint, or flour or powdered chalk for flagging.

Marking a Slope

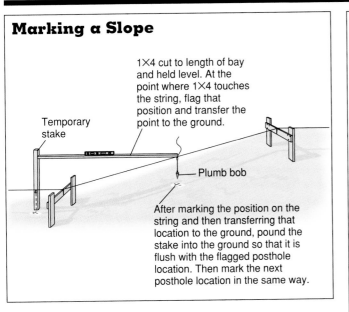

1×4 cut to length of bay and held level. At the point where 1×4 touches the string, flag that position and transfer the point to the ground.

Temporary stake

Plumb bob

After marking the position on the string and then transferring that location to the ground, pound the stake into the ground so that it is flush with the flagged posthole location. Then mark the next posthole location in the same way.

Digging Tools

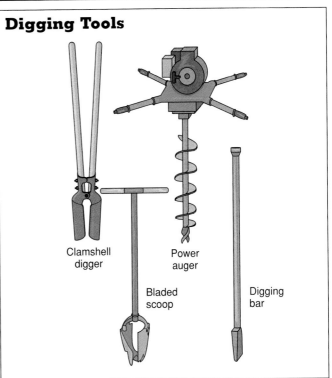

Clamshell digger

Power auger

Bladed scoop

Digging bar

Here's the step-by-step procedure for marking, cutting, and digging postholes:

1. Check the post spacing. Before you assume that the post spacing you've planned on paper will divide up precisely in the field, it's a good idea to double-check. To do this, measure the overall length of each section of fence and compare the figures with those on your plan. Are they the same? If not, you'll need to adjust the fence-line divisions (see page 46 for easy ways to deal with the problem).

2. Measure and mark the posthole locations. The locations are marked on center, from the center of one post to the center of the next. Since the string line indicates the linear center line of the fence, the exact center point of a corner post is where two string lines cross. This is a good place to start measuring for marking the posthole locations. When you've confirmed or adjusted the post spacing, measure along the string line and mark each location by wrapping a little masking-tape flag around the line.

3. Mark the posthole locations on the ground. When all the locations have been marked on the string line, use a plumb bob to mark them on the ground. Flag the spot by poking a nail through a scrap of cloth at the point of the plumb bob, by dropping a handful of flour or chalk there, or by giving the spot a spray of nontoxic paint.

When you've completed the job, leave the batter boards in place; you will soon use them to reestablish the string lines in a new position to guide you in setting and aligning the posts. Cut a little V-notch in the batter board where the string line now rests (or mark it with an indelible pen) so you can find the right position later. Then untie the lines so you have open access for digging the postholes.

Marking a Slope

You'll use a different technique to mark posthole locations on a slope so they will be evenly spaced according to the run of the slope. (If you measure along the actual grade, they will be closer together than the posts that are on level ground.)

To do this, you'll need to make up a layout stick. Cut a 1×4 equal to the on-center size of the bay. Then drive a tall stake into the earth so its surface is precisely flush with the last posthole location. With the aid of a helper, butt the layout stick against the stake and move it up or down the stake until the mark at the other end intersects the string, and the layout stick is level. Flag the point and repeat the process. Take the stake with you and pound it in at each new position.

Digging the Postholes

Digging postholes is hard work. The more you dig in a day, the more resoundingly this truth comes home. To make the job as easy as possible, choose the proper posthole digging tool for the situation at hand.

Tools

How many holes do you need to dig? If there are quite a few, consider using a power-driven earth auger or hire a drilling firm to do the job. If you have only a few holes to dig, a hand tool will work just fine. In either case, posthole digging tools can be rented at tool-rental outlets, lumberyards, or hardware stores.

If you plan to use a power auger, choose a tool that will give you a hole of the proper diameter for the post size.

Aligning and Bracing Posts

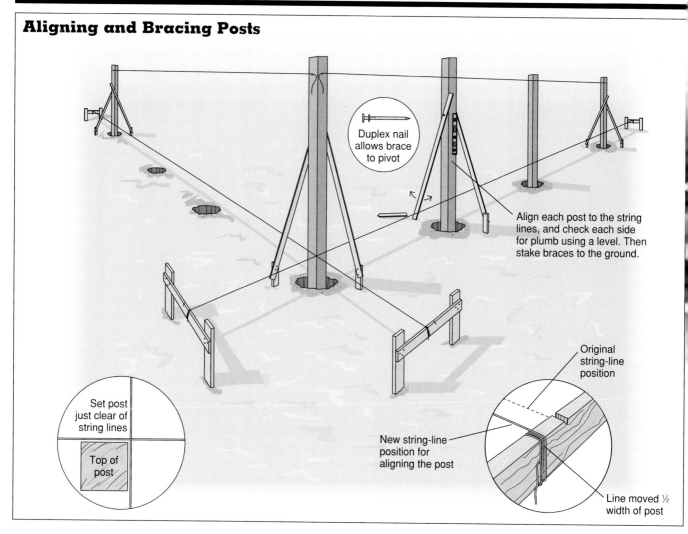

Duplex nail allows brace to pivot

Align each post to the string lines, and check each side for plumb using a level. Then stake braces to the ground.

Set post just clear of string lines

Top of post

Original string-line position

New string-line position for aligning the post

Line moved ½ width of post

One-person augers have a smaller bit than do two-person augers. Bear in mind that power augers have a lot of torque and can be difficult to handle and guide.

If you plan to dig the holes by hand, don't even consider using a shovel. It can't give you the clean, straight-sided hole needed to stabilize the fence posts. For rocky soil, a clamshell digger works better than an earth drill, though the double handles tend to break down the sides of the hole if you need to dig them much beyond 2 feet deep. A steel digging bar helps to loosen the soil and rocks.

If the soil is loose and free of rocks, a single-handled earth drill or a bladed scoop digger will work well. Review the illustration on page 45 to see how wide and how deep each post should be. (Terminal posts—end, corner, and gate posts—are typically larger than intermediate posts and are set deeper.)

Technique

There is no special technique for digging postholes, though the aim is to cut a plumb hole to sufficient depth with clean, straight sides. If you can *undercut the hole* (make it

wider at the base than at the top), all the better: This is the best way to anchor the post in the earth.

Once all the holes are dug, clean out the bottoms so that no loose earth remains. If you're using concrete post footings, clean up the diggings; spread them evenly in surrounding planting beds or cart them away. If you're using earth-and-gravel backfill footings, keep the soil for the mix.

Then shovel about 6 inches of gravel into the bottom of each hole for drainage. A rock in the bottom of each hole makes a solid post foundation;

then add enough gravel to create the 6-inch drainbed.

Setting the Posts

Setting posts is the most important part of the fence installation. If they are plumb and in perfect alignment, you'll breeze through the rest of the construction process. The fence will be upright, handsome, straight, and true. If the posts aren't plumb and are poorly aligned, it means a lot of extra fitting and special cutting to coax the parts together in a sound and attractive way.

If your fence style uses dado or mortise joints to house the rails in the posts, or if the posts have decorative tops (finials), you'll need to set the posts to the exact height (see pages 62 and 63). Otherwise, you don't have to be so careful about the height of the posts, since you will cut the entire line of posts to the proper height later.

Setting the posts consists of the following five phases, all of which are much easier if you don't have to do them alone:

1. Restretch the string lines between the batter boards so they now indicate the outside surface of the fence posts. Measure the actual thickness of the end post (remember, for instance, that a 6×6 doesn't measure a full 6 inches), and divide that measurement by 2. The answer is the distance that you need to move the string line over from its original position.

2. For each section of fence, you should place, plumb, and brace the end posts in their holes. Stand an end post in the hole and twist its base into the gravel bed about 2 inches. Add a couple of braces (1×3 or 1×4 boards) about two-thirds of the way up the post on two adjacent faces. These need to pivot, so use only one nail per brace (a duplex nail is easy to remove later). Then, with the aid of your helper, plumb the post on two adjacent faces with a 2-foot level. One person holds the post in position while the other aligns and plumbs it. When everything is just right, pound a stake firmly into the earth next to the bottom of each brace, and use a couple of box nails

Installing a Tubular Metal Fence

Tubular aluminum and steel fences are available in a wide variety of sizes, designs, and colors. Typically, they are sold as kits, complete with posts, rails, prefabricated panels, and hardware. You may need to supply only some concrete for the footings and a few basic tools. The illustration here shows a common installation, but you will want to follow the manufacturer's exact recommendations.

Note that this fence is constructed one section at a time. First, the end or post is set in concrete. Insert mounting brackets into the rails and then screw them to the post. Next, set an intermediate post in the next hole, attach the rails with their mounting brackets in place, then pour concrete in the posthole. The gate should be hung with the brackets and fasteners included in the kit.

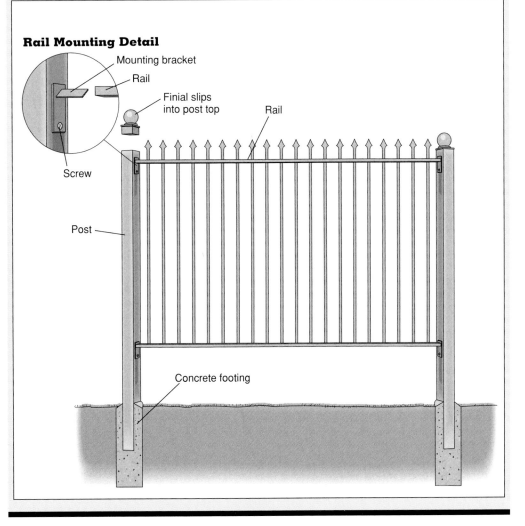

Rail Mounting Detail
- Mounting bracket
- Rail
- Finial slips into post top
- Rail
- Screw
- Post
- Concrete footing

to fasten the brace to the stake. Repeat the process for the post at the other end.

3. Place, align, and brace the intermediate posts. When both end posts are aligned and braced, stretch another string line between them about 18 inches below the top of the posts on the same face as the first string line. Now proceed down the line, placing, aligning, and bracing each successive intermediate post, just the way you did for the end posts. The string lines will help you position them accurately, but don't let the posts touch the strings. Intermediate posts are smaller than end posts, so the string can indi-

61

cate when the post is aligned, but if the post were to touch the string, it wouldn't be centered in the hole.

4. When all the posts are braced, set them permanently in their footings, either earth-and-gravel or concrete (see illustrations below), one by one down the line. Double-check each post for alignment and plumb.

Setting a Post in Gravel

Setting a Post in Concrete

Earth-and-Gravel Footings

The key to making the posts fully secure in this type of footing is to tamp vigorously each successive layer of backfill once it's placed in the hole. The best tool to use for tamping is the shovel handle. It fits easily in the hole, punches the backfill down tight, and the weight of the shovel blade adds extra heft to each tamping stroke. You can use the end of a 2×2 or a 2×4 if that's easier for you to manage. Overfill the hole so that you can cap it, with the slope from post to earth. This helps the footing shed water rather than having it collect around the post where it will promote rotting. You can strip the braces from the posts when you've finished setting the footing; but if they don't obstruct the mounting positions of the rails, take advantage of the extra strength by leaving them in place while completing the frame.

Concrete Post Footings

Whether you mix the concrete from scratch (1 part cement to 3 parts sand and 5 parts gravel) or from premixed sacks, the batch should be stiff and able to pack into a ball in your hand. You will have about 20 minutes before the mix begins to set up and get rigid. Make sure the bottom 2 inches of post are embedded in gravel before placing concrete in the hole. Then, by shovelful, place the concrete in the hole; poke it with a pipe or a broomstick to work out any air pockets. Overfill the hole at the top and crown off (slope) the concrete to keep water from collecting around the post. Use a trowel (a spatula or pancake turner from the kitchen will also work). Leave the braces in place until the concrete has set up and cured. If the braces aren't in your way, you can leave them in place for extra support even as you add the rails.

Fixed-Height Posts

If you are using posts with mortises or dadoes, or with finials that preclude cutting them to height after installation, you will need to set the posts precisely to height. Figure out how much post you want to have above the ground, then measure down that distance from the top of the end post. Fasten a pair of cleats at that point (as shown here), and position the post in its hole. Plumb, align, and brace it; then repeat for the other end post.

Stretch a string line over the tops of the posts and adjust them until the string is level. Then set the remaining posts, using the string line to gauge the proper finished height.

Fixed-Height Posts

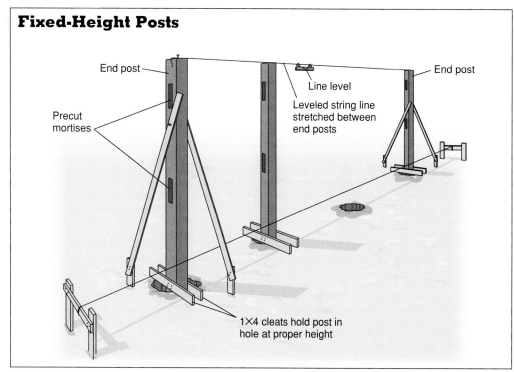

End post

Precut mortises

Line level

Leveled string line stretched between end posts

End post

1×4 cleats hold post in hole at proper height

Cutting Posts and Adding Rails

If you set the posts at random heights, now is the time to cut them to length. This procedure is done in three phases:

1. Snap chalk lines on the line of posts to mark the placement positions for the rails.

2. Install the top rails—marking, cutting to length, and nailing them to the posts one by one until all are in place.

3. Install all the bottom rails, using the same techniques.

So now it is time to put on your nail belt and fill the pouches. The secret to a fence's longevity and appearance is a generous use of nails, especially at this stage (see Nailing Techniques and Patterns at right). Follow the instructions and illustrations below:

1. Measure and mark the posts for cutting height. On your elevation sketch, see how tall the posts (not the infill) should be. From the ground, measure up the post to the proper height and mark that point on the yard-side face of one end post. Fasten a nail at that point and secure a chalk line to it. Run the chalk line out to the other end post. If the fence is on flat ground, use a string to adjust the chalk line; pull it taut and snap it. If the fence is on a slope, measure up the end post to the proper height and snap the chalk line there. Make sure all posts are marked; you may need to resnap the line.

2. Mark each post with cut-off guidelines. For posts in level ground, and for posts that will form stepped frames,

Marking Posts for Cutting

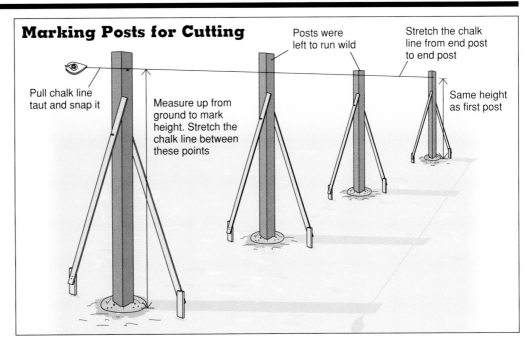

Pull chalk line taut and snap it

Measure up from ground to mark height. Stretch the chalk line between these points

Posts were left to run wild

Stretch the chalk line from end post to end post

Same height as first post

Nailing Techniques and Patterns

For rails that overlay the posts, either on flat or on edge, use a four- or five-nail pattern, as shown at right. All are face-nailed. With spanning rails, stagger the nails to prevent splitting the board. For rails that butt between the posts, use a six-nail pattern. All the nails are toenailed.

To make nailing easier, start the nails first, then position the rail, and hammer the nails all the way in. If you find the nails split the lumber, blunt the point of each nail a bit before starting it.

Blunting Nails

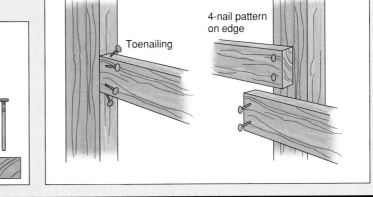

Nailing Patterns

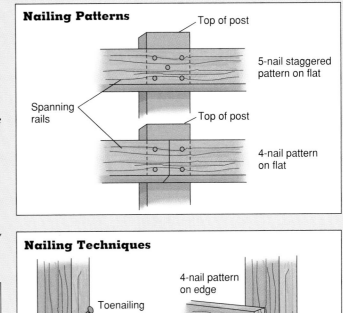

Top of post

5-nail staggered pattern on flat

Spanning rails

Top of post

4-nail pattern on flat

Nailing Techniques

Toenailing

4-nail pattern on edge

use a try square to carry the chalk lines around the post. (For stepped frames, the chalk line will be angled. Use the lower end of the line as your starting point. Using a try square, carry it across the downhill face. Duplicate the angled line on the opposite side; ignore the higher end.) For posts that will form stepped frames, simply cut off the post at the indicated chalk-line angle. If you need guidelines on all four faces to help you make an accurate cut, just carry the lines around so they indicate the cutting angle.

3. Cut each post to height with a handsaw or a hand-held power saw. Use a ladder to be able to see the guidelines, and hold the tool in a safe and comfortable position.

4. Drill a pilot hole in the center of the post, then screw the finial into place, if you are decorating the post tops with prefabricated finials.

5. Add the rails. Distribute the rails around the perimeter of the fence line so the assembly can move more quickly. Remove the braces if necessary. Always measure the rail positions from the top of the posts down. Measure the placement positions of the top and bottom rails on each end post and fasten a nail at those points. Run a chalk line between those points and adjust it for level, or correct its angle. Then pull it taut and snap it. For stepped frames or for sloped frames over uneven terrain, the rail positions for each successive pair of posts will have to be measured and marked separately. For frames on level ground or on an even slope, you can mark an entire

Carrying Marks

Chalk mark carried

Snapped chalk line

Saving the Line

Marked cut line

Saw just to the outside of the marked cutting line; that way the length of board you marked is the length of board you get

Attaching the Finial

Pilot hole

Installing the Rails

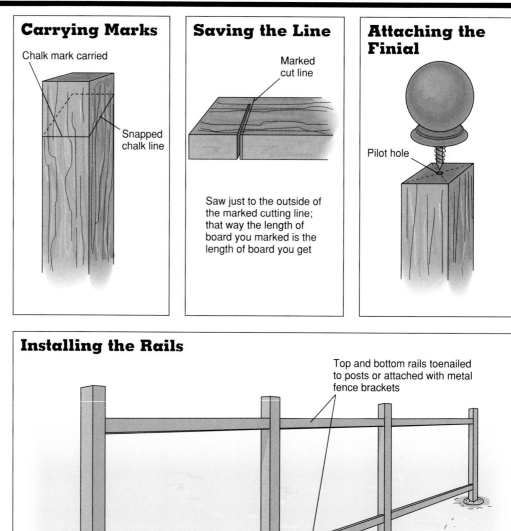

Top and bottom rails toenailed to posts or attached with metal fence brackets

Chalk line shows you where to place the rail for fitting and installing

Fit the rails by holding them in place and marking the cutting lines where the rail intersects the posts

section of the fence line at once by snapping a continuous chalk line.

6. Mark and cut top rails to length and nail them in place. There are two ways to

mark the rails to be cut to length: use a measuring tape, or hold the rail in position and mark it. Then cut the rail to length and nail it in place. If you use the second marking

technique, the rail should be held to the posts exactly where it will be mounted and in the proper position, either on edge or on flat. (Be sure when you cut the rail to length that you save the line—cut just to the outside of the marks—so that get a snug fit.) Work your way around the fence, marking, cutting, and nailing all the top rails in place.

7. When the top of the frame is tied together, go back and mark, cut to length, and nail the bottom rails in place. When the frame is complete, strip away any bracing that remains and clean up the debris.

Adding the Infill

You have now arrived at the best part of all; your idea takes shape in final form. Adding the infill seems like the fastest, easiest part of the installation, no matter how much or how little nailing it requires. After all, the end is now in sight, and since the processes repeat, you can build up a good rhythm and speed and still work with skill.

Because there are so many styles of infill, and each one is treated a little differently, this section presents the subject in its two broadest categories: nail-on and inset. Most types of infill can be mounted either way, depending on the finished effect you want.

Look at both processes, and review the tips, techniques, and guidelines illustrated and described on the following pages. Then follow the installation instructions that apply to the style of your choice.

Nail-On Infill

Nail-on fence styles are faster to build than inset fences; and depending on which face you see, the surface looks quite different—though both

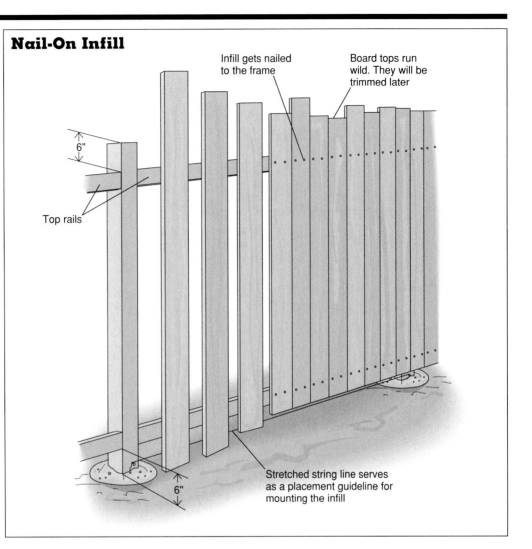

Nail-On Infill

Infill gets nailed to the frame

Board tops run wild. They will be trimmed later

6"

Top rails

6"

Stretched string line serves as a placement guideline for mounting the infill

can be attractive. For this type of infill mounting over level earth, you don't need to pre-cut the infill to length (unless the tops have a cut detail, as pickets and grape stakes do). You can let the board ends run wild—be of random heights—at the top and later cut them to a finished line all at once. Here is how to do it:

1. Distribute the infill materials around the perimeter of the fence line so it's close at hand when you start to install it.

2. Nail tack strips or stretch string lines between posts to act as placement guides for the bottom edges of the board.

(You can do this about three or four bays at a time and then move them up to the next series of bays when you get there.) If the terrain is evenly sloped, guidelines here will help you; but if it is uneven and you're running the infill along the contour, just eyeball the placement of the bottom edge of each successive board.

3. Begin mounting the infill at the end, corner, or gate post. Nail it up board by board until all the infill is fastened in place. Every 3 or 4 feet, use a level on the edge of the last board to make certain that the infill is plumb. If it gets out of plumb, correct the discrepancy

by adjusting the placement of the next few boards.

4. When you've finished, measure and mark the cutoff line along the top edge of the fence, at the end of each section. Snap chalk lines between those points. This chalk line will be the cutoff line if you use a handsaw. If you use a hand-held power saw, measure down from the chalk line a distance equal to the blade's offset from the edge of the saw's shoe. (See page 68 for an illustrated example of this process.)

5. Tack on a cutting guide strip (1×3s, for example). Make sure the joints are even

so the saw's shoe doesn't catch and make a jog in the clean, finished top line you cut.

6. Cut the fence line to height and clear the yard of the debris.

7. If you are staining or painting the fence (and didn't do so before installation—see page 55), prepare surfaces according to the manufacturer's instructions. To protect your landscaping, cover surrounding plantings and earth with plastic tarps.

Inset Infill

Fences with an inset infill require more careful construction than nail-on styles do, but they return a special beauty for the effort. Inset fences look clean lined and gracefully refined, and they show an equally attractive face on both sides. The infill material can be precut to size, as long as you are sure that the opening is in square and of a standard size. Here are the steps:

1. Measure the height and width of the opening of several bays, or all of them if you think there might be discrepancies in size or squareness.

2. Check for squareness by holding a framing square in the corners of each bay, or measure the diagonals (if they're equal, the opening is perfectly square). If the opening isn't square, it won't show if board placements receive extra care; just let them absorb the discrepancy equally throughout the bay. (Rigid sheet materials can be cut to fit exactly.)

3. Precut the infill materials to length, both boards and nailing strips. Note that you

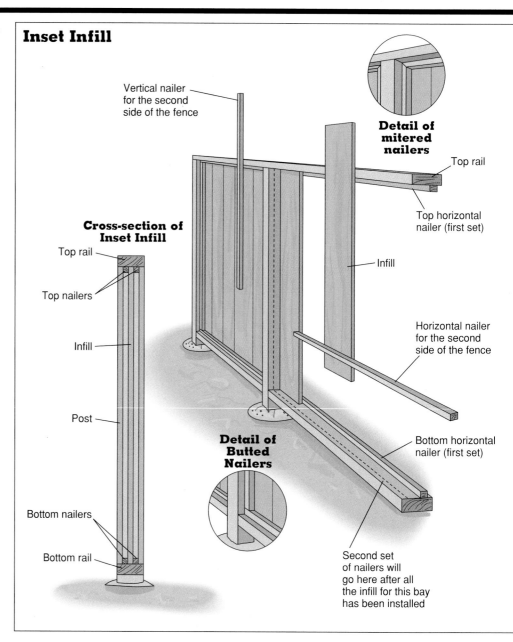

Inset Infill

Vertical nailer for the second side of the fence

Detail of mitered nailers

Top rail

Top horizontal nailer (first set)

Infill

Horizontal nailer for the second side of the fence

Bottom horizontal nailer (first set)

Cross-section of Inset Infill

Top rail

Top nailers

Infill

Post

Bottom nailers

Bottom rail

Detail of Butted Nailers

Second set of nailers will go here after all the infill for this bay has been installed

can miter the strips for a special visual effect, or you can butt them against each other; in the latter case, let the crosswise pieces extend the full width of the opening. The upright pieces will fit snugly between.

4. Measure and mark the nailing-strip positions at a few points on each side of the frame. (You'll install the set of strips toward the outside of

the fence first. This will give the boards a surface to rest against as you nail the infill in place.) Use a box of finish nails to fasten the strips to the frame.

5. Toenail the infill boards to the frame, not the nailers, working from one side of the opening to the other. Occasionally, using a level, check the edge of a board for plumb. Correct any discrepancies by

adjusting the placement of the next few boards.

6. Toenail the other set of nailers to the frame to cover the boards' unfinished edges. When you have completed all the bays, clean up the debris.

7. Prepare surfaces according to the manufacturer's instructions, if you're planning a finish treatment. Protect the landscaping with plastic tarps.

Techniques for Installing the Infill

The tips, techniques, and guidelines on these pages will make the job of installing infill faster and easier, and the fence will look better for it. To make sure the infill is well fastened to the frame and is able to resist loads such as weather, wind, and general wear and tear, use plenty of nails or fasteners. Keep the following tips in mind when you install the infill.

•Keep boards plumb. To do so, check the infill every few feet with a 2-foot level. If the infill has gotten out of plumb, correct it by leaving small compensatory gaps between pieces until the discrepancy is corrected.

•Keep spaces between pieces of infill even and regular. Make a spacer, which will save you from measuring for each piece of infill. The cleat hangs in on the top rail, freeing your hands to hold the infill in place as you nail.

•Keep the angled infill even. Use a bevel square or make a template to properly position the infill to the frame.

•Keep bottom edges flush and smooth. Use guidelines to help you gauge placement at a glance—unless your design intentionally calls for a random effect. You can stretch string lines between posts to guide you. Or tack a 1✕3 or 1✕4 to the surface of the posts, so the infill has something to rest on while you nail it in place. Reposition the tack strips every few bays as you work your way down the line.

•Finish a top edge that was left running wild. Measure

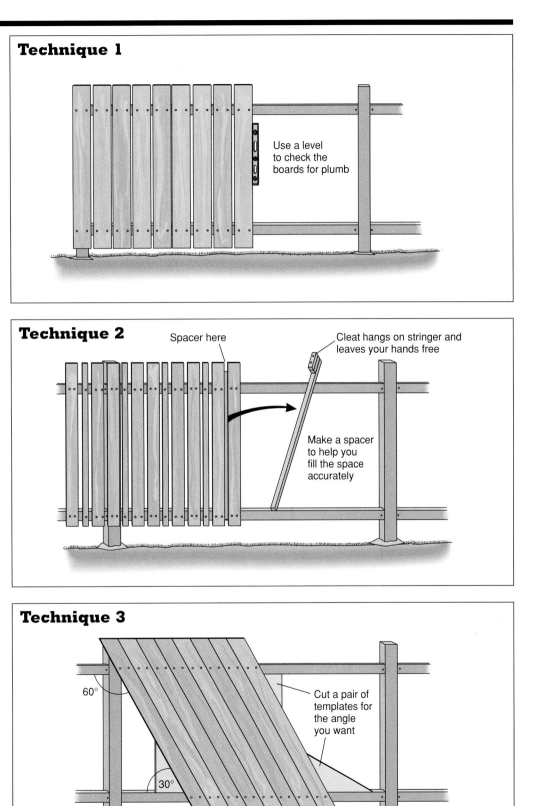

Technique 1

Use a level to check the boards for plumb

Technique 2

Spacer here

Cleat hangs on stringer and leaves your hands free

Make a spacer to help you fill the space accurately

Technique 3

60°

30°

Cut a pair of templates for the angle you want

Bottom Edges Flush

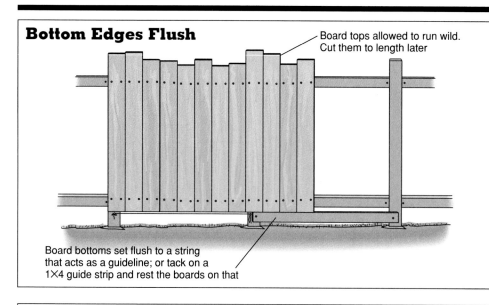

Board tops allowed to run wild. Cut them to length later

Board bottoms set flush to a string that acts as a guideline; or tack on a 1×4 guide strip and rest the boards on that

Finish a Top Edge

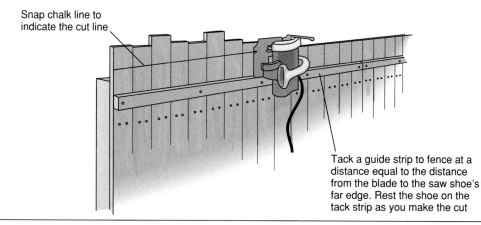

Snap chalk line to indicate the cut line

Tack a guide strip to fence at a distance equal to the distance from the blade to the saw shoe's far edge. Rest the shoe on the tack strip as you make the cut

Installing Kickboard

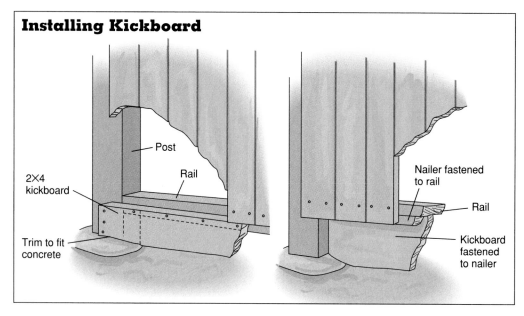

Post

Rail

2×4 kickboard

Trim to fit concrete

Nailer fastened to rail

Rail

Kickboard fastened to nailer

and mark the cut line using a chalk line. Then lightly tack on a series of 1×3 or 1×4 cutting guides at a distance below the chalk line, equal to the distance from the saw's blade to its shoe. Set the blade to a depth sufficient to cut through the infill, but no deeper. Rest the saw on the cutting guide and cut the entire top of the fence off in one pass.

•Install kickboards. Overlay kickboards on the posts or inset them to the underside of the bottom rail and attach to a nailer. Use pressure-treated lumber, or all heart, or a decay-resistant species, since the board touches the earth and is, thus, subject to rot. Kickboards are used to close the gap at the bottom for a more finished look and to keep animals from crawling under the fence.

Adding to an Existing Fence

It's easy to add new sections of fencing to an existing fence; simply determine the sizes of the parts—posts, rails, and infill—and build the new one to match the old.

The only crucial point is the one at which the new fence meets the existing one. The better they're fastened together, the more they'll work in tandem to bear the shared loads.

New sections of fencing will look best if you duplicate the wood species and finish of the existing fence. If the fence has weathered, the new sections will stand out until the weathering process

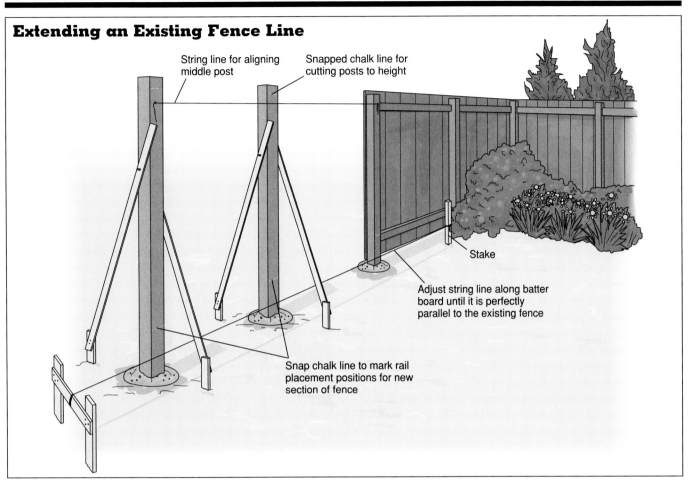

Extending an Existing Fence Line

String line for aligning middle post

Snapped chalk line for cutting posts to height

Stake

Adjust string line along batter board until it is perfectly parallel to the existing fence

Snap chalk line to mark rail placement positions for new section of fence

catches up. But you can diminish the brand-new look by using quick-weathering techniques and finishes. For example, on some species of wood, the application of stains or other chemical mixtures can weather it almost instantly. Choose a stain that matches the weathered tone of the existing fence. By the time the stain wears off, the fence will have weathered sufficiently underneath it to make it harmonize with the old. If the fence is painted, repaint the old part when you paint the new. Finally, if the old fence has weathered naturally, you can make it look nearly new again by applying a bleaching product.

Planning the Layout

The construction processes are the same ones used to build new fencing. First, take field measurements and plan the extent of the new section.

If you want to experiment with different layout options, you might want to make a rough sketch of the area you're considering (see pages 12 to 16). Then, to design the fence, measure the sizes of the existing fence members, the post locations, and the relationships of all the parts—rail positions, special details, and so forth.

Determining Materials

To learn how much of each type of material you will need, make a sketch of what the fence will look like (one bay will be enough) and then compute the number of linear feet of material you'll need for each fence part for that one bay. Then multiply to determine the totals you'll need to complete the entire new section.

Extending an Existing Fence Line

Pound a stake into the ground about 6 feet before the end of the old fence and about 1 inch away from it. Pound a batter

board into the earth about 4 feet beyond the length of the new section.

Tie a string line between these points, adjusting it along the batter board until it is an even 1 inch from the existing fence and exactly parallel to it. Measure and mark the posthole locations on the string and on the ground; then flag them.

Adding a Perpendicular Section

Start the new section at an existing post. There, you can fasten directly into it the new rails for the first bay. If this conflicts with your design, plan to add a new post; you'll

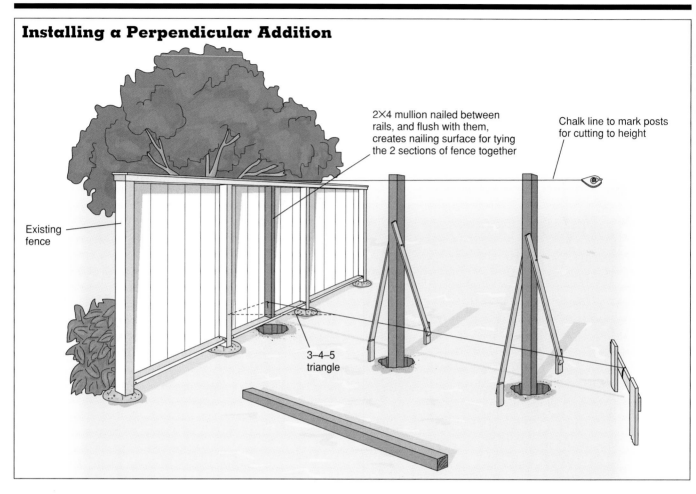

2×4 mullion nailed between rails, and flush with them, creates nailing surface for tying the 2 sections of fence together

Chalk line to mark posts for cutting to height

Existing fence

3–4–5 triangle

also need to add a *mullion*, a midbay upright, between the existing rails so that you have a good fastening surface for it.

Pound a batter board into the ground about 4 feet beyond the end of the new section. Stretch a string line from the existing fence to the batter board and square it up using the 3–4–5 measuring triangle (see pages 56 to 58). Measure out and mark your new post locations on the string line and then on the ground (see pages 58 and 59).

Dig the postholes, set the posts, and add the rails and infill just as you would do for new fencing (see pages 59 to 68). If your fence section includes a gate opening, remember that gate posts should be larger than intermediate posts and should be set deeper in the earth (see page 45).

Preserving the Fence

Surface finishes have a wonderful way of transforming a lot of little pieces into a unity of parts—a single element that blends with the whole site design. Because the finish you choose might affect the type of material you purchase, think about finishes early.

Choosing the Finish

Stains and paints give the fence protection and certainly transform its appearance as well. Sealers don't appreciably change its appearance, but they do provide protection. Bleaching treatments, on the other hand, give no protection but they change the look by speeding up natural weathering processes and lightening the natural wood tones.

As you consider surface finish treatments, you will want to focus on color, tone, and surface sheen (from flat to glossy), degree of durability and protection, and ease of application. You'll also want to make sure that products are compatible with one another and with the fence material itself, and that they are within your budget. Your material supplier will be able to help you choose finish products.

Sealers

Sealers, or water repellents, are clear or lightly pigmented finishes that seal the wood against water penetration. A simple, clear sealer may slow the graying process of wood, but it will not stop it.

Sealers are available with a range of additives to increase their effectiveness. Since water is not the only enemy that wood faces, preservatives are added to protect against mildew, insects, and fungi. UV blockers are added to sealers to maintain the natural color of the wood. Pigmented sealers will provide all of this protection while slightly changing the color of the wood, as well. All-purpose sealers generally contain water repellents, preservatives, and UV blockers.

Sealers keep bleaching treatments from taking effect unless you wait about two months after applying the sealer before applying the bleaching agent. Sealers can be applied to stained wood. They can be used under stain, primer, and paint for extra protection. Make sure the products you use are compatible with each other.

Primers

Primers penetrate the wood's surface and provide some tooth so the paint will stay bonded to it. Primers also make paint application faster. For best results, all surfaces of the wood should be primed.

Oil-based (alkyd) primers are the best choice for raw wood. They adhere to the wood better than do water-based primers. They may need to be thinned with solvents, and they are more trouble to clean up. Redwood and red cedar have extracts that tend to dissolve and bleed through the paint coat. The best way to avoid this is to use an oil-based primer with stain blockers. An oil-based primer works fine under water-based paint.

Water-based (latex) primers are easy to clean up and less expensive than oil-based products. They should not be used on redwood or red cedar.

Paints

Paints look clean, crisp, fresh, and architectural and are an appealing counterpoint to natural surroundings, especially if they borrow the color themes of the dwelling. Painted finishes tend to last longer and look better on smooth surfaces than on rough ones. Paints form an opaque film on the surface of the wood, so they can conceal defects in lower-grade lumber to create a very handsome finished effect, an advantage that stains can't offer. They can also be periodically recoated. However, paints are more expensive and require more care in application.

There are two categories of paints to choose from: exterior alkyds, which are oil-based products (more costly, more difficult to clean up, and take longer to dry), and exterior latex paints, which are water-based (less expensive, easy to clean up, and quick to dry). Each type is available in a range of colors and surface sheens (gloss, semigloss, and flat or matte). A good-quality acrylic-latex top coat applied over an alkyd primer is a good choice for a durable fence finish.

Stains

Stains have a blander finished effect than do paints, but they allow a fence to harmonize with both the landscape and the architecture. Stains are easier to apply than paints are because they require no undercoat. They go on easily over both rough and smooth surfaces. Semitransparent stains are particularly suitable for highlighting the beauty of wood grains. Heavy-bodied (or solid-color) stains resemble paint in their opacity, but because stains penetrate the wood's surface (rather than forming a layer over it), they cannot actually conceal defects. Stains are somewhat less expensive than paints and take less time to apply.

Stains come in two categories: water-based and oil-based. Each category offers differences in opacity, ability to penetrate the wood's surface, durability, and cost. Oil-based stains are especially recommended for redwood and red cedar. Stains don't offer much variation in sheen; they tend to retain the wood's natural look.

Heavy-bodied stains contain more pigments and generally emulate the effects of paint more fully than do semitransparent stains. Semitransparent stains allow more of the wood's natural grain to show through, but they do wear away more quickly than heavy-bodied stains. Make sure products are compatible with one another and with the wood.

Bleaching Treatments and Weathering Stains

Bleaching treatments offer an intermediate solution to the jarring appearance of a brand-new fence. They soften the raw wood look and blend in the fence quickly—as nature would have done after a season or two. Bleaches work by interacting with the elements. Some products might be harmful to landscaping—a possibility you will want to consider. Because sealers inhibit bleaching action, be sure to read the section on sealers on page 70.

If you want to quickly weather the fence, use a stain that will make the wood look like it's already weathered. As the stain wears off, the wood will have weathered and the differences won't be very apparent.

Applying the Finish

On a new fence, the quickest and easiest way to apply a finish may be to do so before the fence is built (see page 55). If you decided to wait until the fence was installed, follow these instructions.

Let the fence dry for a few weeks before applying any finish. Dry wood absorbs much more than does wet wood. For best results, give the entire fence a good cleaning. Mix 1 cup household chlorine bleach per 1 gallon water, then scrub the fence with a fairly stiff brush and rinse. If the fence has weathered naturally for some time and you would like to restore the original wood color, use 1 part bleach with 3 parts water. You can also use special wood-cleaning products (often sold as deck cleaners).

Before applying the finish, read the product's instructions for recommended methods of application. Most finishes can be applied with a brush, pad, roller, or multipurpose pump spray. For larger projects, an airless sprayer may be the best choice, but only if you've taken the time to practice on scrap wood, and you spray the fence on a windless day. For applying sealers, a good quality roller with a 1-inch nap will give quick and thorough coverage. Note that most clear sealers should be recoated while still wet.

Building Special-Purpose Fences

Swimming Pool Fence

The National Safety Council says that drowning is the second leading cause of accidental death in children under three years old. A properly built swimming pool fence will go a long way toward minimizing such a tragedy in your pool. It should be secure enough to prevent children from climbing over or slipping through, and it should allow good visibility from the outside into the pool area—chain link and clear acrylic are good choices for fence material. Check with your local code department to see what laws might apply. The American Fence Association and the U.S. Consumer Product Safety Commission have set minimum standards for designing pool fences, which should be followed in conjunction with local codes.

Dog Fence

How high can your dog jump? Your fence should be at least a couple of inches higher. As a general rule, large dogs should be enclosed by at least a 6-foot fence; smaller dogs require about 4 feet.

And how deep can your dog dig? Many a plan for securing dogs has been foiled by their ability to dig. For best results, bury the fence at least 6 inches to discourage the underground escape route.

Invisible fences, usually sold and installed by specialized contractors, are often used to keep pets from straying. A wire is buried along the boundary, and the dog wears a special collar that sends a tone and then a shock when the dog approaches the wire. Particularly nervous or aggressive dogs may be undeterred by the shock, however.

Security Fence

Many city dwellers have found that the fence they built to keep out potential burglars offered burglars a means to hide from neighbors instead. A security fence should permit good visibility from the outside (wrought iron, tubular steel, and chain link are good choices), be high enough to discourage prowlers (at least 5 feet high), and tough to break through (metal is better than wood). It should have a gate that locks securely. A motion-sensing light near the gate can offer security and safety. Check with your local police department for more advice.

Windbreak Fence

Contrary to common sense, the best way to fence out the wind is not to build a solid fence. Better protection is offered by a fence that allows some wind to pass through. For optimum effect, the fence should be built perpendicular to the prevailing wind. A louvered fence, especially if the louvers are horizontal and angled down toward the inside of the fence, is best (see page 28). If wind is a serious factor, a row of tightly spaced trees may be preferred. Until they are grown, however, you can install a fence of special polyethylene netting, which is designed specifically for blocking the wind.

Snow Fence

Snow comes from the same direction as wind, and a good windbreak fence can help keep down the drifts. Don't put the snow fence right next to a driveway or sidewalk. Keep it at least as far away as the fence is high.

Wire-bound wood slat fences (see page 31) can effectively control snow drifts. They can easily be erected early in winter and taken down in the spring. However, researchers have found that the Wyoming snow fence is a better solution. It has horizontally installed 1×6 rails spaced 6 inches apart, creating

If your present fence is not adequate for keeping dogs in (or out), attach 4-foot wire fencing or hardware cloth to it. Bury the bottom of the fencing at least 6 inches in the ground.

an ideal 50 percent porosity. A 10-inch gap at the bottom prevents extensive drifting at the fence line, which can quickly bury a fence and render it useless.

Deer Fence

The most effective way to keep deer from entering your yard is with a fence that is too high for them to jump. The minimum height is 8 feet. You can construct the fence from any fencing material, but the most economical material, especially for long fences, is 4-inch woven-wire fencing (use a smaller size mesh if smaller pests, such as rabbits, are also present). Attach the wire fencing to T-posts, which are 10-foot metal posts with metal attachments on the bottom. Set the posts 2 feet into the ground, 10 feet apart. Use wooden 4×4s for corner posts. Attach the wire fencing to the posts with wire. Secure it to the ground with wickets or bury it a few inches.

If an 8-foot-tall fence is too unsightly, you can build a slanted fence 6 feet high and angled so that the top is offset 6 feet from the bottom. Ordinary poultry wire will do for the fencing. It should be 8 feet wide, which may mean attaching two sections of 4-foot-wide wire together. Set wooden or metal posts 8 feet apart. Attach the netting to the tops of the posts, pull the bottom of the netting outward at a 45° angle, like one side of a tent, and secure it to the ground with wickets or metal stakes.

Swimming Pool Fence

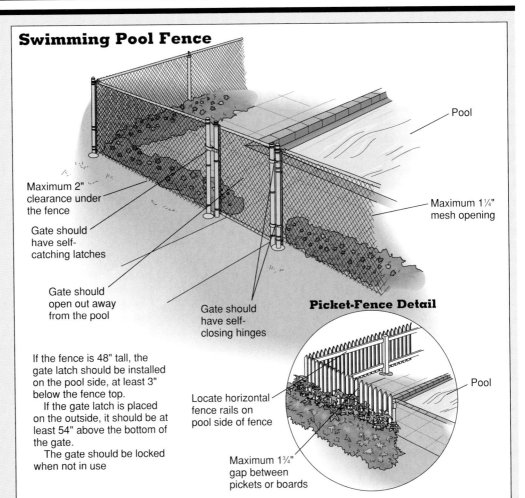

Pool

Maximum 2" clearance under the fence

Gate should have self-catching latches

Gate should open out away from the pool

Gate should have self-closing hinges

Maximum 1¼" mesh opening

If the fence is 48" tall, the gate latch should be installed on the pool side, at least 3" below the fence top.

If the gate latch is placed on the outside, it should be at least 54" above the bottom of the gate.

The gate should be locked when not in use

Picket-Fence Detail

Pool

Locate horizontal fence rails on pool side of fence

Maximum 1¾" gap between pickets or boards

Wyoming Snow Fence

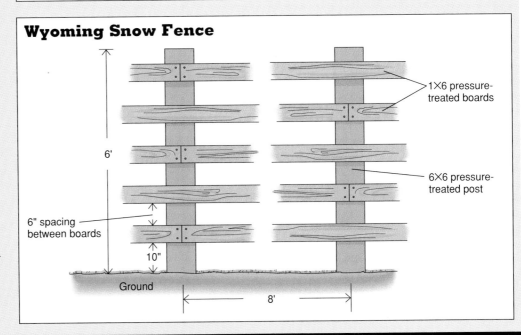

1×6 pressure-treated boards

6×6 pressure-treated post

6'

6" spacing between boards

10"

Ground

8'

Installing a Chain-link Fence

Chain-link fences don't get much respect. But if you need a fence principally for security—to provide security around a swimming pool or to keep kids or pets in the yard—and you want a long-lasting solution that requires virtually no maintenance, then a chain-link might be your best choice. Building a chain-link fence is not difficult. You should be able to buy all the materials and rent all the tools you need from a fence supplier.

Chain-link fencing is readily available in 4-foot, 6-foot, and 8-foot widths. The mesh is woven from 6-gauge to 11-gauge (6-gauge is thicker, and thus stronger) galvanized steel, although you can also find vinyl-coated fencing in a variety of colors. There is also a choice in the size of the mesh opening—wider is cheaper, but smaller is more difficult to climb. A maximum opening of 1¼ inches is recommended for swimming pool fences (see page 34) unless it's woven with wood or plastic slats.

Lay out the fence line and set posts in concrete (see pages 56 to 62). Terminal posts are larger than intermediate posts and come equipped with different fittings. Posts should be evenly spaced and no more than 10 feet apart. After the concrete cures for several days, install the tension bands, end band, and a post cap on each of the terminal posts, and a loop cap on each of the intermediate posts.

Install the top rails carefully through the loop caps and into the end bands. Rail sleeves are used to join sections of rail. Unroll the chain-link mesh along the outside of the fence. Slide a tension bar through the end row of mesh and secure it to the tension bands. Move along the fence line, loosely attaching the mesh to the top rail with tie wires. Slide a stretching band (or another tension bar) through the mesh about 3 or 4 feet from the next terminal post. Attach the fence stretcher to the stretching bar and terminal post, and tighten the mesh until it is taut. Remove extra mesh, slide a tension bar through the end, and secure it to the tension bands. Tie the mesh to the top rail and posts.

To install the gate, first attach the gate fittings to the gate posts, then hang the gate in the gate hinges. Finally, set the gate latch.

Installing a Chain-link Fence

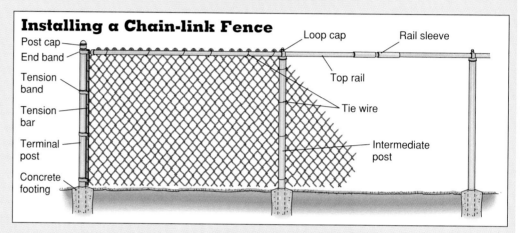

Post cap
End band
Tension band
Tension bar
Terminal post
Concrete footing
Loop cap
Rail sleeve
Top rail
Tie wire
Intermediate post

Using Stretching Bar

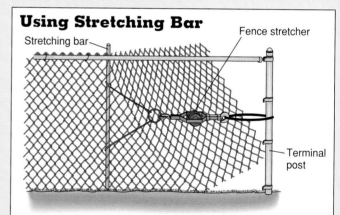

Stretching bar
Fence stretcher
Terminal post

Gate Installed

Gate latch
Gate supports

REPAIRING FENCES

Most structural deterioration begins with the posts—at grade or below it where the problem can't be seen. Posts not only bear the weight of the fencing but serve to keep the structure vertical and true by transferring wind, wear, and weather loads down to the ground.

As posts become weakened or thrown out of alignment by environmental forces, they can't do their structural job properly. This can result in a skewed or tilted fence, rails that pull away from the posts, and infill that splits or twists loose from the framework. None of these problems will go away if left alone, so treat fence maintenance as preventative medicine. If you give the fence a checkup in the spring or fall, while the ground is loose but not muddy, you'll probably be able to extend its life.

A Fence Checkup

Fences can lose their structural strength in more than one way. Posts can rot out; their footings can crack, loosen, or deteriorate; or they can simply give out due to improper alignment when the fence was built. Wood can split, nails can loosen, termites can become established.

Rot

For concrete footings, use an ice pick or screwdriver to poke around the base of the post. For earth-and-gravel backfill, dig down about 6 inches around the base of the post to check for rot.

In either case, if the wood is soft or spongy, rot has set in

and the post will need to be repaired or replaced before it further weakens the fence. Look for rot at the connections between rails and boards or pickets.

Plumb Posts

If the posts aren't plumb, the fence won't be. If posts begin to tilt a little, the forces of nature will amplify that action, loosening and skewing them until the rails eventually pull away from the posts and the infill pulls free from the framework. To correct this problem, realign and reset the posts, refasten the rails securely, and nail down the infill or siding. Vigorous plants working their shoots into existing fencing can also force joints apart. Cut them away from the fence and renail the joints.

Surface Finish

Fences not only look better but wear better when the finish is able to repel moisture and rot. If the fence has a painted or stained finish, re-coating can add longevity to the fence. If it has been treated with a sealer, drop some water on a horizontal section. If the water beads, the sealer is still functioning. But if the wood absorbs the water, it's time to reapply the sealer.

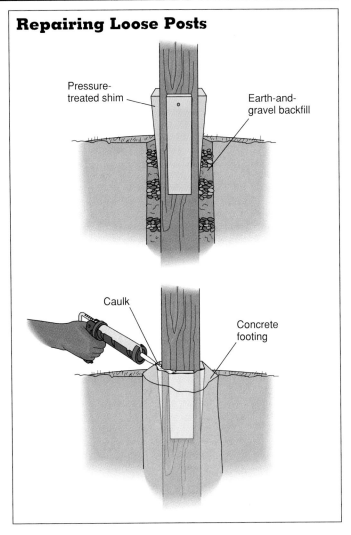

Repairing Loose Posts

Pressure-treated shim

Earth-and-gravel backfill

Caulk

Concrete footing

Fasteners

Over time, nails and screws can loosen. Inspect all the connections on the fence, and tighten any loose fasteners. If a nail won't seem to tighten in its hole, try a larger nail or screw.

Loose Posts

If the post was set with earth-and-gravel backfill, you may be able to steady it by driving pressure-treated shims into the ground on each side of the post. Nail the wedges to the post, then tamp the earth around the post. If the post is

too loose for this treatment, dig out the backfill and set the post in concrete.

If the post in a concrete footing is loose, drive pressure-treated shims into the concrete on each side of the post. Trim off the protruding shims, then run a bead of caulk around the top.

Decayed Posts

If the post was set with a concrete collar, use a wrecking bar to break up the concrete and remove it. If the post is set in a full concrete footing, you will need to remove the old footing first. This will be much

Mending Decayed Posts and Leaning Fences

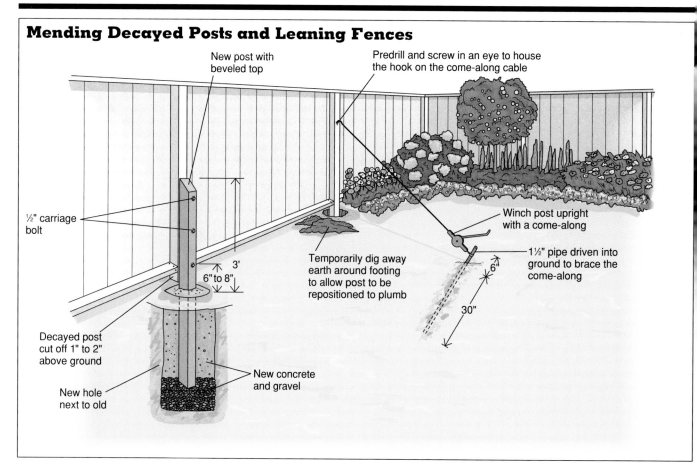

New post with beveled top

Predrill and screw in an eye to house the hook on the come-along cable

½" carriage bolt

3'

6" to 8"

Temporarily dig away earth around footing to allow post to be repositioned to plumb

Winch post upright with a come-along

1½" pipe driven into ground to brace the come-along

6"

30"

Decayed post cut off 1" to 2" above ground

New concrete and gravel

New hole next to old

---

easier if you dig the new post-hole next to the footing, then wiggle it free and pull it out. If the post was set with earth-and-gravel backfill, dig it out. Then follow these steps to replace the post:

1. Without detaching rails or siding, cut away the old post about 1 or 2 inches above ground level, or as close to that point as sound wood remains. Clean out the hole, taking care to keep its sides as straight as possible. If the fence is badly skewed or tilted, you can work it back upright bit by bit with the help of a *come-along*, a winchlike tool available at rental outlets.

2. Put 6 inches of gravel in the bottom on the hole. Cut a length of post (pressure-treated or the heartwood of

a decay-resistant species) so it will extend about 3 feet above the earth. Cut the top of it to a 45-degree angle so it can shed water.

3. Place the post in the hole, work it several inches into the gravel bed, and mark bolt positions so that the lowest bolt is 6 to 8 inches above ground—or above that if the wood isn't fully sound to that point.

4. Drill holes to accept ½-inch galvanized carriage bolts, and securely fasten the two sections of post together. Plumb the fence, if necessary, and brace it in place. Add concrete and crown the top. When the concrete has set, remove the braces.

Rotted Rails

Rotted rails can be resecured to posts in a number of ways. Nail a 2×4 support under the rail, or attach a corner iron or T-plate to the post and rail. Apply caulk to the joint.

A Leaning Fence

If part of a fence is leaning or skewed, either because posts have rotted or because earth movement has forced the structure out of alignment, you may be able to add new midspan posts to reposition and support the fence. Follow these steps:

1. Brace the fence with 2×4s so it doesn't fall over. Then dig out the earth or break out the concrete collars around the errant posts so you

can right the fence. Don't remove any stringers or infill. These are key parts of the fence, which you want to keep intact as much as possible.

2. To pull the fence back into alignment, work in stages. Pull the fence a little at the end posts, then at the next posts, then the next, and back again, bracing each amount of gain you achieve. To do this, use a pulley or a come-along. Both are available at tool-rental outlets.

3. When the fencing is upright and braced in a plumb position, determine the on-center position for the new midspan posts. The repair will be most unnoticeable if you put the new posts at the exact center of each existing bay.

Repairing Rails

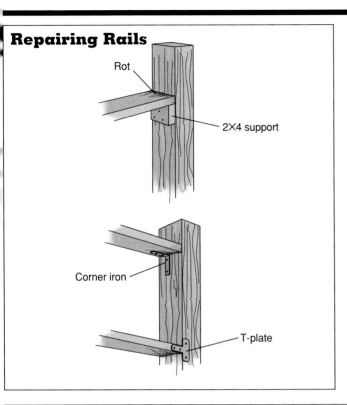

Rot

2×4 support

Corner iron

T-plate

4. Measure and mark posthole locations, then dig them out with a clamshell digger. Place the holes so the new posts will be centered in the holes and notched in to stand flush with the existing framework.

5. Shovel 6 inches of gravel into the bottom of each hole. Place the post in the hole and work it about 2 inches into the gravel bed. Plumb it and mark the notching positions on both the rail and the post. (Each will receive half of the other to make a tight, flush joint.)

6. Notch both the new midspan post and the existing rail, and nail the new post securely in place. Check for plumb, and adjust the bracing as needed.

7. When all posts are braced and nailed, fill the postholes with concrete and crown the footings with a slope so they shed water.

8. When the concrete is fully set, remove the bracing and renail any loose rails or infill that may have worked free. Don't use the same nail holes. If the wood is dry, it may split as you nail, so drill pilot holes first, using a bit slightly smaller than the nail's shank.

9. At the base of the fence, saw off and remove the remains of any deteriorated posts and refill the holes with the dirt from the new ones. Restain the new posts or give them quick-weathering treatment to make the repair less noticeable.

Adding a Post Midspan

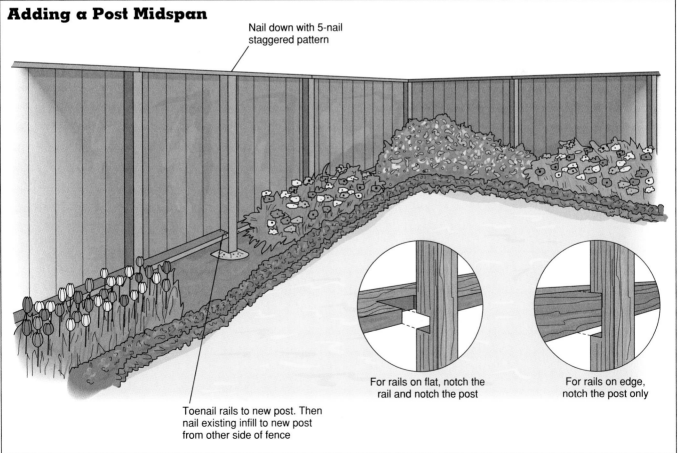

Nail down with 5-nail staggered pattern

Toenail rails to new post. Then nail existing infill to new post from other side of fence

For rails on flat, notch the rail and notch the post

For rails on edge, notch the post only

BUILDING AND INSTALLING GATES

There's something magical about a gate. Each one seems to have a unique character, some special quality about it that people recognize, come to know, and enjoy. It's impossible to say how or why something as simple as a gate can become a memorable acquaintance. Just what is it about a gate that engenders such affection?

Maybe it's because gates and gateways promise an experience—a transition from that place to this one, a leaving behind of what was, a stepping into what will be. There is a bit of magic in every gateway—even those that have grown rickety (having carried one too many children astride) and now sag or squeak or drag. These gates have endured, been treated gently, been carefully repaired and renewed. It's no wonder, then, that gates win our appreciation.

This well-crafted gate structure will last many years. The posts, set in concrete, are pressure-treated for ground contact. The framework for the overhead pergola is securely connected with carriage bolts, and the 2×3 slats have blocking between them to minimize warping. The sturdy gate is designed to resist sagging. The gate's hinges, latch, and spring have a corrosion-resistant finish for outdoor use.

WHAT KIND OF GATE?

Gates can be a focal point, punctuating the entry or highlighting some special area on site. Or they can be concealed to look like part of the fence. They can mirror the lines of the fence and yet counterpoint the style by using similar materials in a different way. Or they can be made from entirely different materials.

Creating a Spirit and Impression

There's a lot you can do with a gate; and it, in turn, can do a lot for you. It can create an image, project an impression, and signal with a silent language how you would like others to approach it. A tall, solid, locked gate gives no permission to enter, save to those who hold the key. But a little painted picket gate that spans a path with modest charm lets those who approach know that it is ready and willing to welcome them in. Some gates stand open, ceremonious and on reserve—others, sentrylike, on guard, signaling to those who pass through to state their business. Some are strictly utilitarian; others are whimsically fantastic and free.

And there are those gates that are arbored or canopied, that extend you a protected welcome with fanfare and verve. Each one gives a message and reflects something of the nature of the place. There are many ways to design a gate so its spirit and impression are just right.

Depending on their purpose and the impression you'd like them to give, some gates warrant more visual importance than others. A main-entry gate, for instance, might deserve a more prominent design than would a gate that leads into a service yard. A gate can draw a lot of attention to itself, or none at all, depending on its design and material.

A gate can completely contrast with a fence. A metal or wooden gate of a different style from the fence announces its presence like an actor on center stage. By design, this gate treatment interrupts the fence line's visual continuity to highlight its place in the scheme of things.

A gate can match a fence exactly. Those that do, detail for detail, effectively conceal the fact of their existence. When you want to downplay the gate, a hinged one that is mounted flush with the fence surface will be discreet.

A gate can also harmonize with the fence in style, but have distinguishing special effects, such as an openwork top or a particular trim detail. This invites attention to the gate without detracting from the visual continuity of the fence line.

This gate repeats the same pattern of bamboo and wood used for the fence.

The 1×1 pickets used in the fence are also used in this gate, but in a different arrangement.

Gates can say many things, from a simple "Keep out" (top left) or "Come in" (top right), to a bold artistic statement (bottom).

In planning and designing your gate, the first step is to choose its material—wood or metal. A wood gate and a wood fence are a naturally pleasing combination, whether you buy a prefabricated gate or design one yourself. A metal gate and an ornamental iron fence are an enduringly attractive combination. However, a metal gate in a wood fence needs special consideration. It will look best if used as a counterpoint to an essentially solid-surfaced wood fence, classic and tailored, or in any style that is simple, rectilinear, and clean lined.

Metal gates can be custom designed and fabricated (check your yellow pages under *Ornamental Iron*), or

purchased prefabricated in stock sizes and styles. Appearance, quality, and price vary according to the gauge and type of metal and the size and design of the gate.

Designing the Gate

For all its seeming simplicity—merely an operating section of a fence—a gate is a fairly complex structure. Planning a gate requires careful thought, just as building it requires careful precision. Successful gates function smoothly and look good, even into old age, by taking advantage of the principle of teamwork.

Three separate teams are at work in a fence:

• The gate: Adequate framing and bracing, appropriate joints, and well-fastened infill.

• The hardware: Hinges and screws or bolts, latches, catches, and locks, all sturdy enough to bear their load.

• The fence: Appropriately sized gate posts in sufficiently deep holes, set with stable footings to transfer the load of the gate to the earth.

The task of the gate is to keep itself together. If the gate is too weak or too wide to structurally support its own weight, the fence and hardware must bear the extra burden.

The hardware is pivotal. Its job is to connect the gate to the fence. Hardware that is forced to bear a heavier load than it is able to will become

overstressed, weaken, and lose its connecting grip.

The fence has to stay out of the way but provide support. Its job is to accept the load the hinges pass along and to transfer it to the ground. To the extent that each part of the team does its own job well, the whole system is the better for it.

As you design the gate, keep in mind that its style—the infill and special details—are secondary issues. Any type of infill can be mounted on a frame to create the look you want. The primary design issues you need to address are the structural ones. They must be solved in sequence, beginning with the question, How wide should the gate (or gates) be?

This gate is set back far enough from the steps for it to be opened safely.

Who wouldn't enjoy coming home to a classic garden gate with a vine-covered arbor?

A Gate Is a Structural System

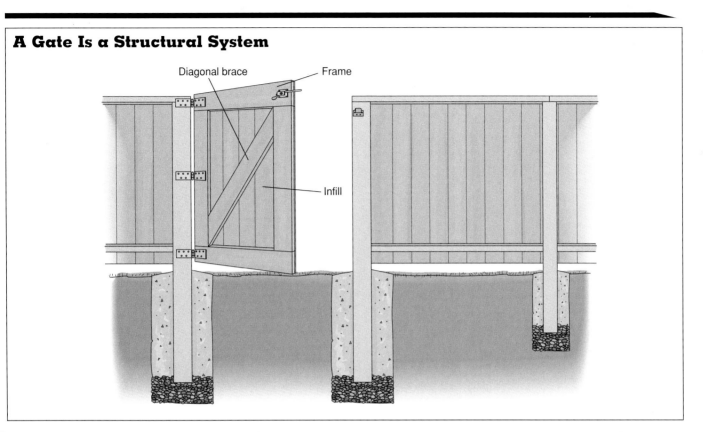

Diagonal brace • Frame • Infill

The Structural System

The style of the gate aside, its strength depends on its structural design, and its durability depends on how well it is built. In order for the gate to operate freely, it must be built square and be sturdy enough to stay that way. In addition, gates place a heavy load on adjacent sections of fence. To bear this load, gate posts are typically made of larger stock and set deeper than intermediate posts. Finally, to join the parts of the system, you'll need to choose appropriately sized and designed operating hardware. See pages 89 and 90 for examples of latches, catches, hinges, and other gate accessories.

The Width of the Opening

If a gate is too wide, it will be in danger of sagging out of square from the sheer load of its own weight. Tried-and-true tradition says that 4 feet is about the limit for a typically hinged, unsupported gate.

If the fence opening is wider than 4 feet, you have two options: you can span the opening with a pair of gates, or you can span it with one very wide gate that has extra supporting mechanisms—a supporting wheel or a wire-and-turnbuckle assembly.

The Swing of the Gate

The illustrations here show you how the location of the gate and the site conditions there will help you determine the direction in which the gate should swing. If you'd like it to swing in both directions, certain types of hardware allow the gate to do this. See pages 89 and 90 for an overview of the different kinds of gate hardware.

At the Edge of Your Property

At the Edge of Your Property

Gates are typically mounted so they swing into the property rather than away from it. In this situation, the gate should swing in one direction only.

Where One Fence Abuts Another

At the Top or Bottom of Stairs

Along a Slope

Across a Hillside

Where One Fence Abuts Another

Gates are often hinged on the side of the fence that's nearest the corner so that views and access through the opening aren't inhibited by the swinging gate. In this situation, it can swing in one or both directions.

At the Top or Bottom of Stairs

If the landing is wider than the arc of the gate's swing, it's safe to mount a gate at the top or bottom of a flight of stairs. People need foot space in which to maneuver the gate, and the landing forewarns that steps exist beyond. In this situation, the gate can swing in one or both directions.

Along a Slope

Gates are mounted to hinge on the low side of the slope so that as the gate swings open, the bottom will clear the slope. Note that the frame is built in square, rather than conforming to the angle of the slope. Though it breaks the visual line of the fence framework, the gate gets the structural strength it needs. In this situation, the gate can swing in one or both directions.

Across a Hillside

Gates are hung so they will swing out toward the downhill direction; the bottom of the gate will swing free and clear of the slope of the hillside. In this situation, it can swing in one direction only.

The Gate-Opening Sketch

The choices and decisions that produce the design of your gate are easy to make, but there are many of them. So many, in fact, that getting them out of your head and down on paper will be a help in making a complete, clear plan before you begin to build.

Make a sketch to scale (1 inch equals 1 foot) of the gate opening and include several feet of fence on either side. Use this as the base drawing. To experiment with alternative design schemes, tape tracing-paper overlays on top of your drawing. This will give you an accurate view of the visual effects for each choice you're considering. It's much easier to build the gate from a plan than it is to make it up as you go along—and the gate is much more likely to fit well and work freely.

Perimeter Frame

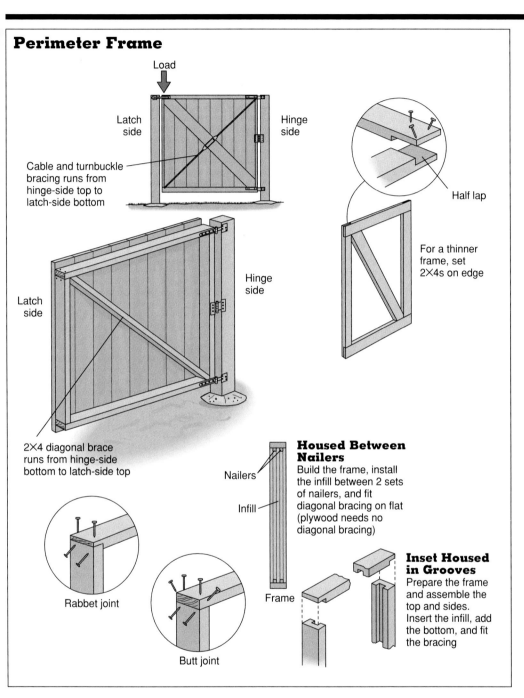

Load

Latch side

Hinge side

Cable and turnbuckle bracing runs from hinge-side top to latch-side bottom

Half lap

For a thinner frame, set 2×4s on edge

Latch side

Hinge side

2×4 diagonal brace runs from hinge-side bottom to latch-side top

Rabbet joint

Butt joint

Nailers

Infill

Frame

Housed Between Nailers
Build the frame, install the infill between 2 sets of nailers, and fit diagonal bracing on flat (plywood needs no diagonal bracing)

Inset Housed in Grooves
Prepare the frame and assemble the top and sides. Insert the infill, add the bottom, and fit the bracing

The Details

Decide first whether you will close the opening with a single gate or a pair; whether the gate will match, harmonize, or contrast with the adjacent fence; and which direction it should swing. To help you decide these issues, sketch out the alternatives on graph paper.

When you have a clear picture of how you want the gate to look, choose the construction details: the framework that joins together the parts of the gate into a single whole and the hardware that makes it operate. In the illustrations above and on page 86, you can see that there are two basic

framework approaches: a Z-frame and a perimeter frame. Look them over and make a sketch or two to decide which one will work best for your gate. Before you decide, consider these factors:

• The two types of frames are comparable in terms of serviceability, but a Z-frame is

generally considered to have less structural strength than a perimeter frame has.

• Both types of frames can take a nail-on infill, but only the perimeter frame can house an inset infill, whether it's boards or a sheet material. (Prefabricated lattice panels, plywood, or plastic infill will look best mounted inset to a perimeter frame.)

• A Z-frame gives a light, casual look, in contrast to the perimeter frame, which tends to look a little more rectilinear and architectural.

After you have decided which type of frame will shape the gate, you're ready to choose the construction details—the joints, stops, and hardware that will join it together.

First choose the joints to assemble the frame; they're shown here in accompaniment to the basic frames. Butt joints are the easiest to build, but they don't offer as much strength as rabbet joints or half-lap joints, which are a little harder to make. Then choose a gate stop, which serves to save the hinges from needless overwork by giving the gate something to close against.

Pages 87 and 88 show you ways to create a gate that matches the fence. Note that the style of the fence can lend a pleasing theme for the gate—a starting point for designing a special character at any transition point. And then, you'll see the basic hardware options. You might want to preview these, too, since the hardware and the frame will work together, both structurally and aesthetically.

Z-Frame

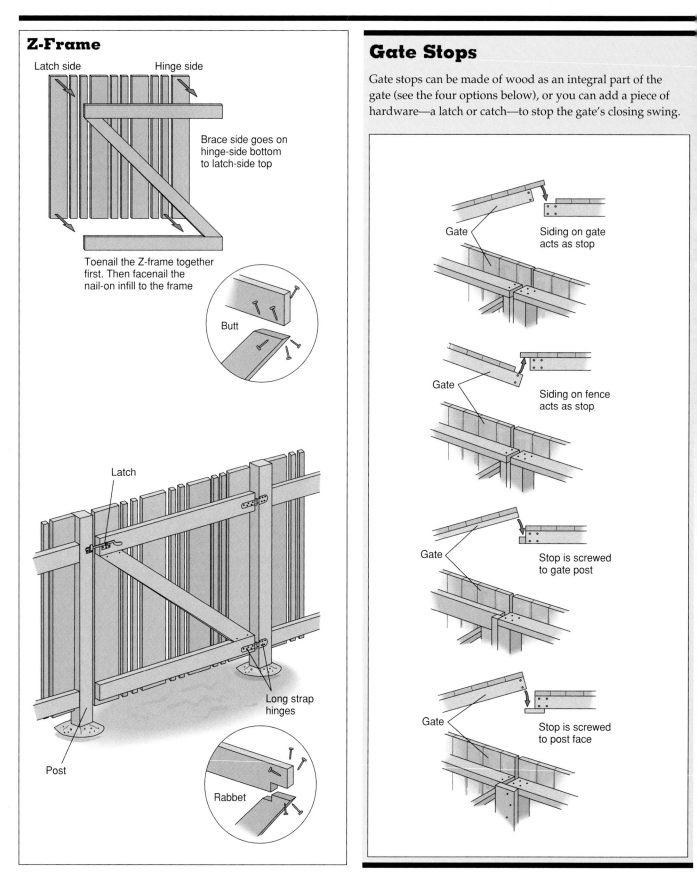

Latch side

Hinge side

Brace side goes on hinge-side bottom to latch-side top

Toenail the Z-frame together first. Then facenail the nail-on infill to the frame

Butt

Latch

Long strap hinges

Post

Rabbet

Gate Stops

Gate stops can be made of wood as an integral part of the gate (see the four options below), or you can add a piece of hardware—a latch or catch—to stop the gate's closing swing.

Gate

Siding on gate acts as stop

Gate

Siding on fence acts as stop

Gate

Stop is screwed to gate post

Gate

Stop is screwed to post face

When you've made your choices for construction details (joints, gate stops, and hardware) and developed the design of the gate, sketch them into your plan. Then make a list of the materials you'll need to complete the gate.

Gate Styles

The following illustrations are examples of a variety of gate designs. If some major elements of the fence—its materials, color, or pattern—are reflected in the gate, that will be enough to tie together the components into a unified whole. The gate designs shown here and on page 88 are influenced by the style of the fence, but they might also depart from it. Yours can, too.

Here (above right), a simple plywood fence, elegantly toned in a classic color treatment, is dressed to the nines with an arched, glass gate. Bright brass hardware adds eye-catching sparkle and works perfectly well in the out-of-doors. Gate posts reach higher than the fence itself to support a lintel, announcing the special place that an entrance is.

If your fence design sports some special detail, such as the raised border cap, shown at right, why not let the gate carry the theme and amplify the whole effect? The openings act like windows to the world beyond, but since they're placed high, the feeling of privacy on the inside isn't at all diminished. And you can't see into the area until you're close enough to the gate to open it.

Arched Glass Gate

Openwork Border Cap

Shingled Wall

Paired Gates

Mixing Materials

A waist-high shingled wall with a contrasting colored cap offers such a pleasant boundary—neither understated nor overwhelming—that a matching gate only enhances the overall effect (top left). Because the gate posts are the same color as the fence cap, the gate itself is clearly visible but remains discreet. And capping the gate to match the fence produces an attractive visual continuity as well.

Even a screen that suggests, but does not enforce, closure can be improved with the addition of a pair of gates to match. Paired gates are just as pleasant standing open, ready to invite passage freely, as they are functional when closed. Because the open fence design shown at left (center) is scaled so large, the only real boundary it produces is a visual one; and gates for this type of screen primarily create continuity for that visual boundary.

Mixing materials is an attractive way to emphasize a gate in a fence line, and metal gates give you an opportunity to do that. Here (bottom left), the gate design takes advantage of the fence style: The square metal pickets are set in a rhythm that mimics the pattern of the adjacent fence. The pickets of the gate remain the same, and the spaces between them differ in width, turning the pattern of the fence inside out.

Gate Hardware

If your eye has ever been caught by a strikingly handsome gate latch or a stunningly beautiful set of hinges, you know what a delightful design element the gate hardware can be. Beautifully designed, carefully fabricated gate hardware is special and also rare. But it's not impossible to find.

The accompanying illustrations give you an overview of the commonly available types of gate hardware (hinges, latches, and catches) in a variety of styles.

If local building supply or hardware sources don't stock what you would like to use, consider having some special hardware made at an ornamental iron shop, or even a brass foundry. Antique shops, salvage yards, stores that specialize in restoration hardware, and your own ingenuity at the workbench might also produce some interesting possibilities.

Clearances

Since required clearances between the gate and gate posts will vary depending on the types of hardware you use, it's recommended that you purchase the hardware before you begin building the gate.

Latches

When choosing a latch, consider ease of operation, security, and whether the design should be formal or rustic. If the gate is tall, your choice is limited to latches that can be operated from both sides of the gate. For security, some latches include locks, or hasps that can be secured with a padlock. Make sure that a

Catches and Latches

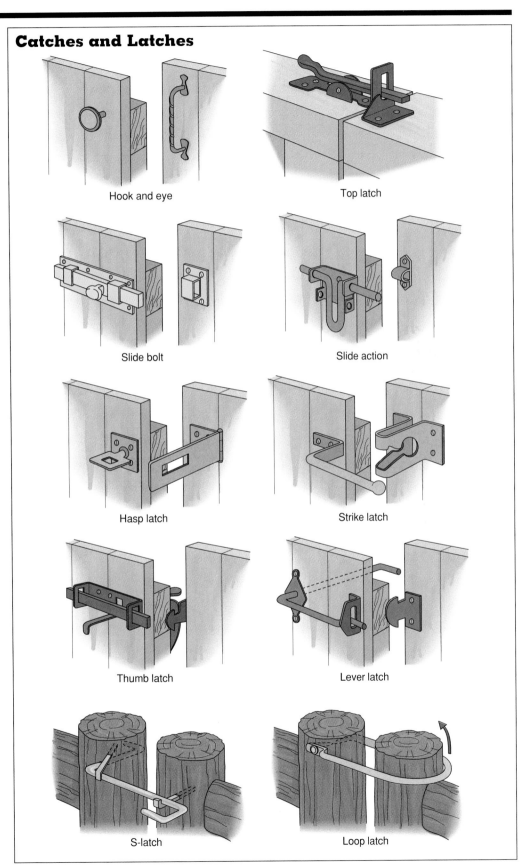

Hook and eye

Top latch

Slide bolt

Slide action

Hasp latch

Strike latch

Thumb latch

Lever latch

S-latch

Loop latch

Hinges and Decorative Hardware

T-hinge

T-hinge

Strap hinge

Butt hinge

Screw hook and strap hinge

Screw hook and eye hinge

Ornamental T-hinge

Strapped H-hinge

H-hinge

Spring hinge

Spring closure

Cane bolt

locked gate can be unlocked from the inside if it will interfere with emergency egress from your property.

Hinges

Regardless of the style you select, remember that even lightweight gates are heavy, and they're subject to the elements and a tremendous amount of wear and tear. Three hinges hang a heavy gate far better than two can. Err on the side of excess when you select the hinges and fasteners—make *heavy-duty* and *heavy gauge* your watchwords.

Screws

If the screws provided aren't long or strong enough to do the job, buy some that are. Screws should penetrate the wood frame as deeply as they can without coming through the other side.

Building and Hanging the Gate

Select each piece of gate lumber carefully; it should be absolutely straight and true. Clear, kiln-dried surfaced lumber is recommended, since it improves the chance of the gate remaining flat and in square despite its exposure to the elements.

The basic construction process illustrated at right is simple and straightforward and can be applied to the building of any gate, whether for a perimeter frame, as shown, or for a Z-frame gate. Here is the sequence of steps, though your own custom design might require additional steps along the way:

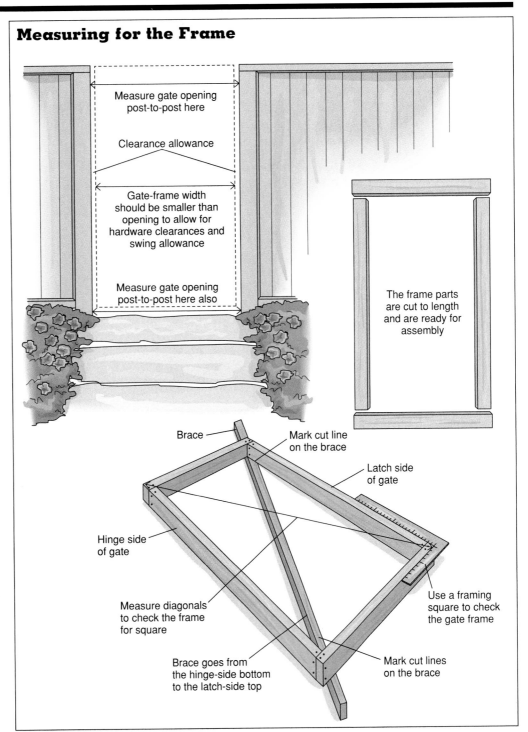

Measuring for the Frame

Measure gate opening post-to-post here

Clearance allowance

Gate-frame width should be smaller than opening to allow for hardware clearances and swing allowance

Measure gate opening post-to-post here also

The frame parts are cut to length and are ready for assembly

Brace

Mark cut line on the brace

Latch side of gate

Hinge side of gate

Measure diagonals to check the frame for square

Brace goes from the hinge-side bottom to the latch-side top

Use a framing square to check the gate frame

Mark cut lines on the brace

1. Measure the opening. Measure the distance between the posts at two points, at the bottom of the opening, and at the top. The measurement for the overall width of the gate consists of this post-to-post measurement, minus the basic (and essential) frame-to-post clearance allowance ½ to ¾ inch), plus whatever additional clearances are required by the hardware you use.

2. Cut the frame parts to length. The cross-members overlay the uprights so water can't readily enter the joint. Cut the cross-members to length, then cut the uprights to fit between them. If using

a special joint detail, prepare the joints now.

3. Assemble the frame. Nail or bolt the frame parts together, making sure that they are properly positioned to each other. A bolted frame is tremendously strong. Nails are apt to work loose, but the assembly can be made stronger with a good application of waterproof glue. The aim is to make the frame flat and in square. To check it for square, measure the diagonals—from the outside corners of the cross-members. If the diagonal measurements are the same, the frame is in square. Use this same measuring technique for a Z-frame to make sure that the parts are properly positioned. Then, lay the frame down on the bracing member, which runs from the hinge-side bottom to the latch-side top, and mark the cut lines. When you cut it to size, save the line—cutting just to the outside of the marks—so the brace will have a tight fit. Toenail the brace to the frame.

4. Add the infill. Put the frame down so that the surface where the infill is to be placed faces you. Is the brace going from the hinge-side bottom to the latch-side top? Make certain it is. Then fasten down the infill and check it for proper alignment as you go. Use the same nailing techniques and guidelines described on page 63 for fences.

5. Mount the hinges on the gate. Measure and mark the hinge positions. Drill pilot holes (make them slightly smaller than the shank of the screw), and fasten the gate leaf of the hinge to the gate.

Gate Infill

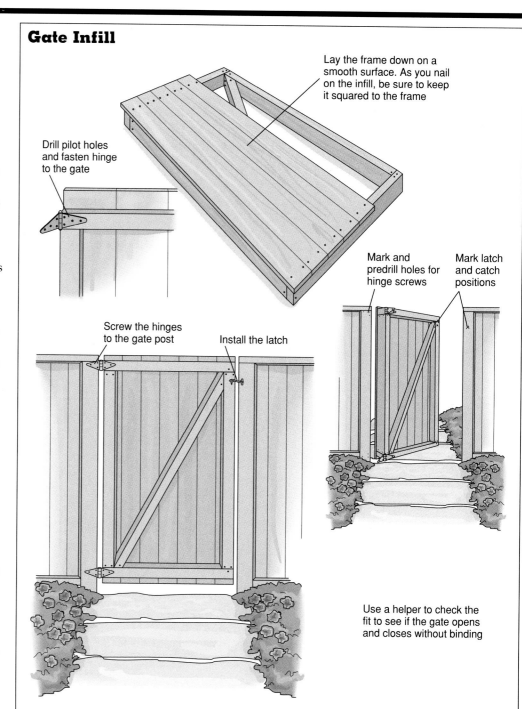

Lay the frame down on a smooth surface. As you nail on the infill, be sure to keep it squared to the frame

Drill pilot holes and fasten hinge to the gate

Mark and predrill holes for hinge screws

Mark latch and catch positions

Screw the hinges to the gate post

Install the latch

Use a helper to check the fit to see if the gate opens and closes without binding

If you're using a wood stop, add it to the post now.

6. Check the fit. Gates, being heavy and a little awkward to handle, are easier to fit with the aid of a helper. Hold the gate in position and see if it will open and close without binding against the post. If necessary, trim the gate to give it clearance.

7. Hang the gate. Prop the fitted gate up in the opening and mark the hinge screw-hole positions on the post. Drill pilot holes and hang the gate. Measure and mark out the latch and catch positions, and mount the hardware on the gate and post. Finish the gate according to your finish treatment plan (see pages 70 to 72 for information about finishes).

GATE REPAIRS

Gates take a lot of abuse. In addition to facing weather extremes, they are pushed, and slammed, and sometimes swung from on a regular basis. Fortunately, most gate repairs are not too complicated.

If Gate Opening Is Out of Square

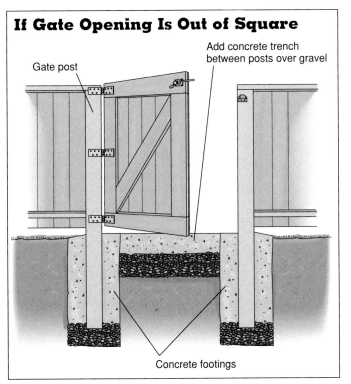

Gate post

Add concrete trench between posts over gravel

Concrete footings

Using Turnbuckle

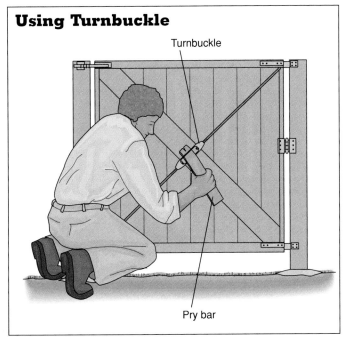

Turnbuckle

Pry bar

Washers and Nuts

Nut

Washer

Bolt

Dowels

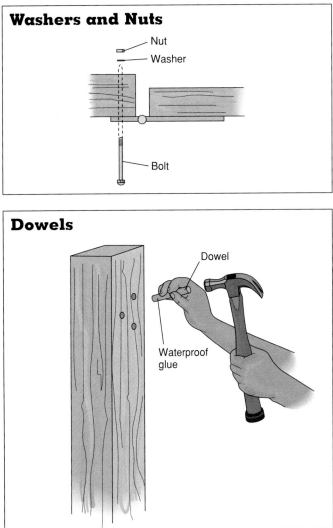

Dowel

Waterproof glue

A sagging gate looks somewhat pathetic and may not open easily or close properly anymore. The cause is usually a loose hinge, an out-of-square gate opening, or an out-of-square gate.

If the hinge is loose, try tightening the screws, or adding larger ones. If that doesn't work, you may want to simply reattach it in a new location. Or you can remove the hinge and plug the screw holes with wood dowels covered in waterproof glue. Then reattach the hinge by driving screws into the dowels. If you can't plug the holes, drill holes through the old screw holes in the post and gate, then attach bolts, washers, and nuts.

If the gate opening is out of square (measure at the top and bottom to find out), the problem is probably loose gate posts. See page 75 for hints on repairing loose posts. If both gate posts are loose, consider tying them together with a concrete trench.

An out-of-square gate can often be righted by attaching a turnbuckle diagonally to the gate, then adjusting it until the gate is square.

RESOURCE GUIDE

Bamboo Fencing

Bamboo and Rattan, Inc.
470 Oberlin Avenue
South Lakewood, NJ 08701
800-4-BAMBOO

Bamboo Brokerage
13245 Woodinville Redmond
    Road
Redmond, WA 98042
206-868-5166

The Bamboo Company
12981 SW 267th Street
Homestead, FL 33032
305-258-5868

Bamboo Fencer
31 Germania Street, Bldg. D,
Jamaica Plain, MA 02130
617-524-6137

Eastern Star Trading
    Company
624 Davis Street
Evanston, IL 60201
800-522-0085

Orion Trading Company
820 Coventry Road
Kensington, CA 94707
510-540-7136

Lumber

American Wood Preservers
    Institute
1945 Old Gallows Road,
    Suite 550
Vienna, VA 22182
703-893-4005

California Redwood
    Association
405 Enfrente Drive, Suite 200
Novato, CA 94949
415-382-0662

Chemical Specialties, Inc.
1 Woodlawn Green, Suite 250
Charlotte, NC 28217
800-421-8661

Georgia-Pacific Corp.
133 Peachtree Street NE
P.O. Box 105605
Atlanta, GA 30303-1808
303-348-5605 or 800-284-5347

Louisiana-Pacific
111 SW Fifth Avenue
Portland, OR 97204
800-547-6331

Quality Forest Products, Inc.
Box 369
Glen Gardner, NJ 08826
908-638-5534

Western Red Cedar Lumber
    Association
1100–555 Burrard Street
Vancouver, BC V7X 1S7
Canada
604-684-0266

Western Wood Preservers
    Institute
601 Main Street, Suite 405
Vancouver, WA 98660
206-693-9958

Western Wood Products
    Association
522 SW Fifth Avenue
Portland, OR 97204-2122
503-224-3930

Metal Fencing

Architectural Iron Company
Box 126
Schocopee Road
Milford, PA 18337
800-442-4766

Cassidy Brothers Forge, Inc.
U.S. Route 1
Rowley, MA 01969-1796
508-948-7303

Custom Ironworks, Inc.
10619 Big Bone Road
Box 180
Union, KY 41091
606-384-4122

Gilpin Ironworks
Box 471
Decatur, IN 46733
800-348-0746

Legi Fences and Gates
OuterSpace Landscape
    Furnishings
7533 Draper Avenue
La Jolla, CA 92037-4894
800-338-2499
619-459-6994

Leslie-Locke, Inc.
4501 Circle 75 Parkway
Suite F–6300
Atlanta, GA 30339
404-953-6366

Moultrie Manufacturing
    Company
Drawer 1179
Moultrie, GA 31776-1179
800-841-8674

Plastic/Vinyl Fencing

B. F. Products, Inc.
Box 6421
Harrisburg, PA 17112
800-255-8397

Bufftech
2525 Walden Avenue
Buffalo, NY 14225
800-333-0569

Calico Supplies
2060 East Indiana Avenue
Southern Pines, NC 28387
800-822-5426

Cross Vinylattice
Cross Industries, Inc.
3174 Marjan Drive
Atlanta, GA 30340
404-451-4531

DuPont Fencing Products
DuPont Canada, Inc.
201 South Blair Street
Whitby, Ontario L1N 5S6
Canada
905-668-5811

Future Fence
P.O. Box 6570
Vacaville, CA 95696
707-449-6301 or 800-794-6575

Hiteck Fence
615 Howard Street
Findlay, OH 45840
419-422-5220

Nebraska Plastics
Box 45
Cozad, NE 69130
800-445-2887

Tensar Polytechnologies, Inc.
1210 Citizens Parkway
Morrow, GA 30260
800-292-4457

Triple Crown Fence
Brock Manufacturing
Box 2000
Milford, IN 46542-2000
219-658-4191

Schwartz's Forge and
    Metalworks, Inc.
2695 Route 315
Box 205
Deansboro, NY 13328
315-841-4477

Stewart Iron Works Company
20 West Eighteenth Street
Box 2612
Covington, KY 41012
606-431-1985

INDEX

U.S./Metric Measure Conversion Chart

	Formulas for Exact Measures Symbol	When you know:	Multiply by:	To find:	Rounded Measures for Quick Reference		
Mass (weight)	oz	ounces	28.35	grams	1 oz		= 30 g
	lb	pounds	0.45	kilograms	4 oz		= 115 g
	g	grams	0.035	ounces	8 oz		= 225 g
	kg	kilograms	2.2	pounds	16 oz	= 1 lb	= 450 g
					32 oz	= 2 lb	= 900 g
					36 oz	= 2¼ lb	= 1000 g (1 kg)
Volume	pt	pints	0.47	liters	1 c	= 8 oz	= 250 ml
	qt	quarts	0.95	liters	2 c (1 pt)	= 16 oz	= 500 ml
	gal	gallons	3.785	liters	4 c (1 qt)	= 32 oz	= 1 liter
	ml	milliliters	0.034	fluid ounces	4 qt (1 gal)	= 128 oz	= 3¾ liter
Length	in.	inches	2.54	centimeters	⅜ in.	= 1.0 cm	
	ft	feet	30.48	centimeters	1 in.	= 2.5 cm	
	yd	yards	0.9144	meters	2 in.	= 5.0 cm	
	mi	miles	1.609	kilometers	2½ in.	= 6.5 cm	
	km	kilometers	0.621	miles	12 in. (1 ft)	= 30 cm	
	m	meters	1.094	yards	1 yd	= 90 cm	
	cm	centimeters	0.39	inches	100 ft	= 30 m	
					1 mi	= 1.6 km	
Temperature	° F	Fahrenheit	5/9 (after subtracting 32)	Celsius	32° F	= 0° C	
					68° F	= 20° C	
	° C	Celsius	9/5 (then add 32)	Fahrenheit	212° F	= 100° C	
Area	in.^{2}	square inches	6.452	square centimeters	1 in.^{2}	= 6.5 cm^2	
	ft^2	square feet	929.0	square centimeters	1 ft^2	= 930 cm^2	
	yd^2	square yards	8361.0	square centimeters	1 yd^2	= 8360 cm^2	
	a.	acres	0.4047	hectares	1 a.	= 4050 m^2	